PRAISE FOR *GRIEF GIRL*

"Fascinating and soberly eye-opening."—*The Bulletin of the Center for Children's Books*, Recommended

"A gripping memoir . . . Glimpses of humor amid tragedy make this a page-turner."—*School Library Journal*

"Any adolescent going through the grieving process will tearfully embrace [Vincent's] book."—*Booklist*

"Her intimate, honest narrative captures both Erin's strength and vulnerability."—*Publishers Weekly*

"An incredible story by an incredible writer."—Ellen Wittlinger, author of the Michael L. Printz Honor Book *Hard Love*

"A treasure for any teenager experiencing grief and loss."
—Rachel Cohn, author of *You Know Where to Find Me*

ERIN VINCENT

grief girl

my true
story

Delacorte Press

Published by Delacorte Press
an imprint of Random House Children's Books
a division of Random House, Inc.
New York

Delacorte Press and colophon are registered trademarks of
Random House, Inc.

Visit us on the Web! www.randomhouse.com/teens
Educators and librarians, for a variety of teaching tools, visit us at
www.randomhouse.com/teachers

The Library of Congress has cataloged the hardcover edition of this work
as follows:
Vincent, Erin.
Grief girl : my true story / Erin Vincent.
p. cm.
ISBN 978-0-385-73353-3 (hard cover) — ISBN 978-0-385-90368-4
(glb edition)
1. Grief in adolescence. 2. Bereavement in adolescence.
3. Parents—Death—Psychological aspects.
4. Teenagers and death.
5. Vincent, Erin.
I. Title.
BF724.3.G73V56 2007
155.9′37092—dc22
[B]
2006011650
ISBN: 978-0-385-73386-1 (tr. pbk.)
Printed in the United States of America
10 9 8 7 6 5 4 3 2 1
First Trade Paperback Edition

To Adam—

this book would not exist without you.

And in memory of Mum and Dad

THANKS TO . . .

Editor extraordinaire Wendy Loggia, who believed in this book when no one else did. Your talent, insights, warmth, and humor made it all so much better. Sara Crowe, my wonderful book-loving agent, who always goes above and beyond. Beverly Horowitz for her much-appreciated support and enthusiasm. Pam Bobowicz for asking all the right questions. Colleen Fellingham for giving it a polish. Angela Carlino for creating a book jacket I adore. The smashing Wade Lucas, my cheerleader and tireless promoter.

Connie, Steele, Theo, and Peter Nounnis, and Venise Damaskos for your love and memories. Julie Price for all the great letters, memories, encouragement, and renewed friendship. Teresa Eather for always being there and for reminding me of things I'd forgotten. Eric Kosse for singing on my answering machine, believing in me, and reading the book when it was 550 pages long.

Marilyn Castro, Sue Chae, Leonora Ribeiro, Francis Sticco, Amanda Youngman, and all my supporters at the bookstore.

Jan Lindstrom-Valerio, Donna Passannante, Miwa Messer, Heather Ryan, Dennis Wurst, and Jennifer Gardiner for being so encouraging. Danielle Assouline, my wise and talented young reader. The fabulous Kim Dower for her generosity, cherished friendship, and wisdom. The gorgeous Judith Nordhal, who always makes me feel like a million bucks. The wise and wonderful Suzanne Wickham-Beaird for sharing so much.

The Society of Children's Book Writers and Illustrators for helping make things possible.

Goddess of goddesses, Agapi Stassinopoulos, for leading me to Harvey Klinger.

Keith Apana, Monica Boggs, Angela Bottrell, Augusten Burroughs, Cherie Courtade, Martin Davison, Kim Delaney, Charles Duncombe Jr., Gigi Levangie, Claudia Harrington (SCBWI), Karen Hebert, Gavin Hignight, Allison Hunter, Toni Lawson, Seidy Lopez, Frederique Michel, Pete Panos, Patti Southern, Austin Storm, Ilka Trevillian, Ken Wilson, Seth Wimmer, and Sian and Nick Worth.

Joanne Steuer, I could not have edited my book without your wisdom and guidance. Thank you for helping me move forward.

Trent and Mayu Jackson for being happy for me. Toni and Kate Haroon for all the fun and laughter back there in Australia.

My gorgeous nieces, Shae, Bree, Michaella, Shelby, Cyan, and Linley . . . just because.

Raelene Roberts, my "adopted sister," and her husband, Scot.

Bradley Knott, Leanna McNeil, and Melissa and Ross Kable for always being there for me and for cheering me on.

My "adopted" parents, Jill and Graham Knott. I could never have done this without your support and unconditional love through the years. Mum and Dad would be so happy to know I have you in my life. There are not enough words to thank you.

And finally . . .

My *Grief Girl* interviewer, transcriber, editor, masseur, cook, cleaner, cheerleader, shoulder to cry on, and most devoted husband in the universe, Adam "love of my life" Knott. You put so much love and hard work into this. This book is yours too. Thank you for making everything possible.

Boy . . . How did I get so lucky?!

TO LOSE ONE PARENT . . . MAY BE REGARDED AS A MISFORTUNE;

TO LOSE BOTH LOOKS LIKE CARELESSNESS.

—Oscar Wilde, *The Importance of Being Earnest,* Act I

I've killed them. Killed them with my thoughts.

Why would I think such a thing?

Am I evil?

Was it a premonition? A daydream? A wish?

Can thinking something make it happen?

October 23, 1983

It's getting late and Mum and Dad aren't back yet. They said they'd be home before dark. So where are they?

I should be happy. Even though I'm fourteen, I've never been allowed to stay alone for more than a few hours, and tonight I've got the whole house to myself. I can blast my music, watch whatever I want on TV, raid the refrigerator. But something doesn't feel right.

This isn't like Mum. She's the kind of mother who'll call and tell me the car has broken down or she's caught up talking to someone, or that she and Dad have stopped for something to eat. She's the kind of mother who worries too much and calls too often.

Maybe I misunderstood. Maybe they said they'd be late?

No, I remember Mum walking over to me on the sofa at lunchtime, kissing me and saying they'd definitely be home before dark.

They were going to visit Nanny's grave in the country, dropping my little brother, Trent, off at Evelyn's house on the way.

So where are they? It's seven o'clock already.

I'll call Evelyn. She's Mum's best friend. "Hi, it's Erin. Have Mum and Dad come to pick up Trent?"

"Not yet. So I get some extra time with him. He's so sweet!"

"Good," I say, distracted. "Um, Evelyn? I'm worried."

But Evelyn tells me not to be. "They probably just got held up, Erin. I'll have them call you as soon as they get here."

"Okay. Thanks."

I hang up. Maybe I *am* overreacting. Mum says I'm a worrywart, but it's her fault. She's the one always going on about wanting to die before us kids. Now she's got me thinking the worst.

Maybe I should do my tapestry to take my mind off things. I've just learned embroidery, and I'm surprising Mum with a tapestry for Christmas. I know it's kind of geeky, but I can't help it. I love how the picture emerges with each stitch. When it comes to her birthday and Christmas, Mum always says, "Just make me something, darling." But I never do.

My sister, Tracy, rolled her eyes when she found out. "You're such a dork. Why do you have to sit around reading all the time? And now tapestry? You're hopeless." Tracy is four years older than I am. We're very different. She says I'm the biggest nerd there is. But I wish she were here now. She's been at her best friend's house all day; they were going clubbing tonight.

It's officially dark. I can see all the neighborhood lights on through our sheer green and cream striped curtains. I probably should get up and turn some lights on besides the reading lamp next to me, but I can't move. I don't know why, I just can't. It's like I'm stuck on the living room sofa.

Just keep stitching and stop it with the stupid thoughts.

I figure if I'm here doing this for Mum, she'll be all right, it will keep her safe. I won't look up. I won't even raise my head. I'll position myself so I can't even see the mirrors behind Dad's bar or the black hole that was the dining room half an hour ago or the kitchen with the echo of the humming fridge making it all seem even emptier. I've never noticed that hum before. Why is it that things sound louder in the dark?

It's eight o'clock. Why haven't my parents called? They should have been home hours ago. Where are they? Where could they be? What if something bad has happened to them? What if they've been in a car accident? What if—

The phone's ringing. Thank God.

5

"Mum?"

"Erin! Is this Erin Vincent?" asks a woman's voice I don't recognize.

My stomach sinks. It's not Mum. I'd better get this woman off quick in case my parents try to call.

"There's been an accident. Your parents have been in an accident!" the woman cries.

I hold the phone tight, trying to process what she's saying. "What? Who is this?"

"Don't worry. I'm a nurse—I'm here with them. Your dad told me to call you."

"I don't understand. What about Mum? What's going on?"

"The ambulance just left, it's on the way to Liverpool Hospital."

"But you said you were a nurse," I say, confused. "Aren't you there now?"

"I'm here at the side of the road. I just happened to drive past."

"Please! What's happened? What's going on? Who are you?" I beg.

"Look, that's all I know. I'm sorry. Call Liverpool Hospital."

"Wait! Don't hang up."

She's hung up! You can't say that and just hang up!

This isn't happening. This isn't happening. This isn't happening.

It was just a prank call. That's it. But how did that

woman get our number, and how did she know Mum and Dad aren't home? How did she know my name?

Oh no. God, no! Please, God, no.

My heart's pounding so hard and fast I feel like it's becoming dislodged from my chest. The threads holding it in place have broken and it's just bouncing around in there.

What do I do?

I pray. *Please, God. Don't let them be dead. I'm begging you. I'll do anything. I'll sing hymns and hand out pamphlets at the mall, I'll watch religious TV. I'll keep you constantly in my thoughts. Just let them have broken legs or arms or something. I know I had that terrible thought last week, but that was just a stupid orphan daydream. Don't all kids think stuff like that?*

It's quiet and dark, but I don't want to put the lights on. My eyes have adjusted and I can see all around me, but it's like someone turned the brightness down on the TV. I'm standing between the dining room and the kitchen. In this light, Mum's expensive wood dining table and maroon-velvet-cushioned chairs look like something out of an old English movie. The copper hood above the stove belongs in the servants' kitchen, where they pluck chickens and stir pots of stew over an open fire.

I need to move. I can't stand still.

I'm walking around the house in circles, around and around and around, faster and faster, until each room becomes a blur. They're dead. Mum's dead. No, what am I saying? She can't be.

She made my lunch today.

I've got to call the hospital. Breathe deeply and think straight. Be strong.

I wish I knew where Tracy was. She's at a nightclub, but which one? Probably better I don't know. Why make her panic too?

These stupid flimsy phone book pages won't turn quickly enough. I'm scared to dial the number but I know I have to. Okay, it's ringing. They're not dead, they're not dead, they're—

"Good evening, Liverpool Hospital," a man answers.

"Oh . . . so this is Liverpool Hospital?" I say, my voice shaky.

"Yes."

"Um, how do I find out if someone's been taken there recently? Tonight, I mean."

"I'll put you through."

"They're okay, they're okay, they're okay," I chant.

"Admissions," says a chirpy voice.

"Hello, I need to find out about two people taken there tonight."

"Names?"

"RonaldandBeverlyVincent."

"You'll need to talk a bit slower," she says. "What are their names?"

"Vincent, Ronald . . . and Beverly Vincent."

Just saying their names makes me want to cry, but I'm not going to.

"Hang on. I'll check."

Please, God. Please. She's going to come back with good news.

She's back. "There's no one been admitted by those names."

"Are you sure? I was told they were going there."

"I'm positive. They're not here."

Is that good or bad? Another dial tone. She's hung up. *Please, God, don't let them be dead.* Where are they? Mum, Dad, come home.

I need to get out of here. Maybe someone else will know what to do. I'll call Auntie Connie, our neighbor. She's not really my aunt, but on my street all the kids call the adults Auntie and Uncle. It would feel strange to call them anything else. Mr. and Mrs. just aren't enough.

Auntie Connie, Uncle Steele, and their kids, Theo, Venise, and Peter, are our closest friends in the neighborhood. They're Greek. Going to their house is like visiting a country within a country, a little bit of Greece just up the road. Having meals there is like going to a Greek restaurant (not that I've ever been to one). We eat with the TV tuned to the *Greek Variety Hour.* Lots of flashing lights and Greek singers and dancers. Venise, Theo, and Peter hate it. I love it.

My hands feel clammy on the phone. Stupid phone.

Theo answers. He's a couple of years older than I am. He's the nicest boy I know. Last year I had the biggest crush on him, but I'm over it now. I tell him what's happened. I'm crying. He tells me his parents are out but that I can come over and wait with him.

I turn off the reading light. Dad will be angry if I leave a light on. I get my keys and lock the front door.

It's a hot and windy Australian summer night. The kind of night in horror movies where bad things happen. But nothing bad would happen on our happy street. It's a cul-de-sac, with lots of kids. We skateboard, have water balloon fights, and ride go-carts down the hill. There's hardly ever traffic, so we never have to worry about being run over in the street, which is a big relief for Mum.

We live in Beverly Hills, thirty minutes from the center of Sydney. It's nothing like the Beverly Hills in America that I see on TV. My Beverly Hills has no rich people. My Beverly Hills has redbrick houses, eucalyptus trees, and Toyotas, not Porsches. I'm going to make it to the real Beverly Hills one day and become a movie star. But in the meantime, the other kids and I perform on the back of Dad's work truck, parked in the street outside our house. We live at number six, which is a lucky number, Mum says.

Please let us be lucky tonight.

I walk up the hill to Theo's and ring the doorbell, and I hear him running down the stairs. He opens the door and the light almost blinds me. Their place is always so bright.

Theo has a strange look on his face. Like he's scared too, or maybe just annoyed. I suppose he had better things to do tonight than comfort me. It's good not to be on my own anymore. We go upstairs to his room and begin to call the hospital every ten minutes. We take turns.

"No, sorry, no one by those names here."

The whole top floor is Theo's domain. His bedroom is off the games room, which has a mirrored bar, a TV, a sound system, and a pool table. Theo, Venise, and I always have so much fun up here. But not tonight.

With every call I'm getting more and more desperate. How can you go missing from an accident to a hospital? It's like my parents have fallen off the face of the earth. Maybe there was no accident. No, no one would be sick enough to play a joke like that, would they?

We call and wait, call and wait.

"Mum and Dad will be home soon," Theo says. He means his. We both know mine might never be home again.

Stop thinking that, Erin!

We call and wait. Call and wait.

"How long has it been?" I ask Theo.

"You've been here for about an hour, I think."

This is driving me crazy. I've got to take my mind off it or I'll give myself a heart attack. That'd be great. We find Mum and Dad are okay with just a few bruises, and I'm dead from the panic of it all.

I've got to think good thoughts, think good thoughts.

There's the sound of a car.

Is it Mum and Dad? Mine, not his? We look out the

window. It's his. Venise is with them, and little Peter is asleep in Uncle Steele's arms. We run downstairs and tell them what I'm doing here.

They put Peter straight to bed and take over.

"Don't worry, Erin, I'm sure everything's just fine," Auntie Connie reassures me, and for the first time tonight I feel like maybe it's not going to be that bad.

"Just sit on the sofa, Erin. We'll take care of it," Uncle Steele says with a smile.

So here I sit staring at the pool table while they make phone calls. Venise is with me, but we say nothing. I'm not moving, but everything inside is. I'm moving without moving.

Uncle Steele's just closed the door to Theo's room. What does that mean?

I can hear murmuring. Do they know something? Are Mum and Dad finally at the hospital or are they on their way home? I don't want to know. What if it's something I don't want to hear? I don't want to wait anymore, but while I wait, nothing's changed. They're both still alive and everything's fine. What if I've waited all this time to hear something awful?

They've found them. I can tell. Auntie Connie just made a terrible *Aaahhhh!* sound behind the door. She's moaning and trying to muffle it. A kind of moan I've never heard before.

No, no, no! *Take it back, God. Take it back. Turn the clock back. Don't let it be.* I want to run but I can't move. I lift my feet off the floor. Don't ask me why, because I don't understand it myself. I just don't want my feet on the floor. They open the door. Auntie Connie looks pale. She's speaking to Theo in Greek and Uncle Steele is walking toward me. He kneels where my feet were.

"They're at the hospital. Your dad is in critical condition," he says with his hands on my knees.

"And Mum?" I ask, wanting, and not wanting, him to tell me.

He just looks at me and I know.

And I run.

Before

Tonight on TV they had people eating each other for dinner.

A group of people were in a plane that crashed in the snow. After several days with no food, they were forced to eat the bodies of the ones who didn't survive.

"I'd do that for you girls, you know," Mum announces. She's ironing in the other room.

"Do what?" I ask from my spot on the floor in front of the TV.

"I'd let you eat me." She pokes her head in. "If we were starving, I'd chop off my arm for you to eat."

"Wouldn't you then just bleed to death?" I ask,

trying not to picture it. This is too much for an eleven-year-old!

Now Dad's listening to us and not the news for a change. "Nah, she could just stick her stumps in the snow and they'd freeze up nicely," he says, smirking. "She'd have a couple of Popsicles for arms."

"Don't play games, Ron. This is serious."

But Dad's on a roll. "Maybe they could suck on your stumps for dessert!"

Mum's always talking about dying. About how she couldn't live if something happened to Tracy or me. She prays God will take her first.

"I couldn't *eat* you. That's gross," I tell her.

"What, you'd just chop them off and expect us to eat them? Just like that?" Tracy scoffs.

"Yeah," Dad says in the breathless wheeze he gets from laughing too hard, "and once you've chopped one off, how will you do the other?"

"God, Mum, you say stupid things sometimes," Tracy tells her. "Anyway, stuff like that doesn't happen in Australia."

Mum looks hurt. "Look, you know what I mean. It's because I love you. That's what I'd do in that situation and that's that."

Mum's been this way ever since Nanny died. Nanny was Mum's mum and was much nicer than Dad's mean old mum, Grandma, who is still alive. As Mum says, "The good people always go first and the assholes live on forever." When it comes to talking about Grandma, Mum stops being a lady.

Nanny was as good as they get. At four foot eleven, she was like a little bread pudding. All warm and sweet and soft. Last year Nanny came to live with us. Actually, she came to die with us; I just didn't know it at the time.

She got breast cancer, turned yellow, and died. Then the ambulance came and Mum went to bed. She just lay there staring at nothing, shaking as if she were colder than cold. I thought she was going to die too.

"Mum, please say something," I'd begged, thinking I could make her better.

"Just give her some time," Dad had said.

So I guess Mum doesn't want to go through that again.

Mum thinks she's fat. So she's become a Weight Watcher. Pretty stupid, if you ask me. How can you lose something if you're constantly watching it? Mum doesn't see it that way. She goes to her meeting every Tuesday.

Last night Mum came home and ran into her bedroom without saying hello. Tracy got up to see what was wrong—she and Mum are "best friends." Tracy likes Mum all to herself, but I wanted to be part of something for once, so I followed.

Mum sat crying on the bed. Next to her on the gold bedspread was a pink rubber pig's head. It was the size of a basketball, with blue eye shadow and long lashes.

"What's that?" I asked, knowing it wasn't meant to be funny.

"Look, Erin, if you have to come in, shut the bloody door," Tracy ordered. She hugged Mum and glared at me over Mum's shoulder.

"They've given me the pig's head," Mum said, weeping. "I'm the worst fat lady in the group. Not only did I not lose weight this week, I put it on! I can't do this anymore."

I pride myself on being good at cheering Mum up at times like this. "Just because you have a pig's head doesn't mean you *are* one."

Tracy shook her head, but Mum started laughing and crying at the same time.

I can relate to Mum better when it comes to this stuff. Tracy doesn't get it because she's skinny. She gets mad at Mum and me for eating fattening food. "It's simple," she tells us. "Just stop stuffing yourselves!"

That's easy to say when you're naturally athletic and beautiful. Tracy's latest school picture looks like a Hollywood movie star's. And she *always* looks that way. I can stare at that picture for hours, hoping I'm half as beautiful when I'm fifteen. Everyone wants to be like Tracy.

Mum's blue passport was on the bed next to the pig's head.

When Dad walks around the house saying, "Where's my passport?" it's because he's threatening to leave us after an argument with Mum. All he does is jump in the car and drive around the block a few times to scare Mum, which it doesn't; instead, it just scares me.

I pointed to it. "Mum, what are you doing with your passport?"

"Ha! I wish that was what it is, darling. It's my Weight Watchers book."

I looked closer. Instead of red stamps from foreign countries, there were little red piggy stamps in it.

"Come on, Mum, throw this stupid thing in the trash," Tracy said, giving the pig's head a slap.

"I can't. I have to take it back next week."

"Well then, let's put it somewhere you can't see it, at least."

"Okay," Mum said, her face blotchy and tearstained.

The next week Mum took the pig's head to her meeting so some other poor lady could go home crying with it.

But Mum was the lucky recipient again.

After her meeting, I heard her on the phone with Evelyn. "I stopped off on the way home and got a milk shake and a Mars Bar. You only live once, right?"

But she doesn't really believe that. Mum believes in heaven and hell, in rubbing Buddha's tummy and that if you're bad, you'll live your next life as a cockroach.

Mum believes in lots of things. Her Bible, her Edgar Cayce reincarnation books, and a little Buddha statue that she moves around the house when the mood takes her. Whenever one of us walks past it, she tells us to rub Buddha's tummy three times in a clockwise direction for good luck. Then there's the tarot lady Mum visits. Mum takes a tape with her each time, but she hides them and won't let us listen. She's into ghosts and spirits as well.

Dad doesn't give two hoots about any of it. He says it's all bullshit.

* * *

Most days, Dad and I are up first. I love our mornings together. We both wake up all chipper and laughing away while Mum and Tracy lie in bed trying to "thaw out," as they call it. I can tell Tracy likes being part of the thawing-out club the same way I like being part of the breakfast club.

Unlike most kids, who have cereal and toast for breakfast, I eat in a five-star restaurant most mornings—if I close my eyes and don't look at the laminated table and ugly brown and orange kitchen.

This morning it's melt-in-your-mouth sautéed beef strips and scrambled eggs. Dad whistles a happy tune as he tosses the beef in the wok and splashes in some sauce before flipping it onto our plates.

We sit together and eat and ooh and ahh. "This is the life," Dad says.

"You make the best stuff, Dad. Why aren't you a chef?" I ask before thinking.

Dad's not smiling anymore. I was just trying to compliment him, but I've said the wrong thing. I do that a lot. Dad dreamed of being a chef, but his father said that was for poofters. So Dad works for a courier company.

"Ughh . . ." Mum and Tracy are up. After what I just said, I'm glad to see them.

Dad smiles again as they groan their way into the kitchen. He and I are a lot alike. We both like to have fun as much as possible. Teasing Mum and Tracy by acting super happy and awake is especially entertaining.

"Hello, you bright sparks!" Dad says, winking at me. My ill-timed comment is forgotten. "Beautiful morning, isn't it?"

I overheard my parents talking about money and our lack of it this year. We're *that* kind of family. One year we're well off and the next we're in the poorhouse. I think it has something to do with Dad's schemes. Our fortune depends on which one he hits on and when. This year it was the gold-panning machine. For months Dad hid in his much-loved three-car (even though we only have one car) garage/workshop inventing a secret machine that would change our lives forever.

"This is going to be it, Bev, I can just feel it," he says when he finally shows us a dark green metal contraption. It's a rectangular box about the size of a sofa with a fat, ridged hose sticking out of one end and a funnel at the other.

"What on earth is it?" Mum asks.

"A gold-panning machine. It can pan in a day what it would take one person a month to pan," he tells us. "The hose sucks up the dirt, which then gets sifted like flour, and any gold in there will come out the other end on the magnetic tray. It's bloody beautiful!"

Mum's trying unsuccessfully to act excited, and I'm trying even harder. I'm thrilled that he might find gold. At the same time, I can't help thinking I have the Nutty Professor for a dad, without the funny genius part. Tracy just says he's a loser.

Dad's a fitter and turner by trade, whatever that is. I should ask him about it, but what if he just fits screws onto bolts and then turns them? A monkey could do that, and I don't want to make him feel bad, because I know he's really smart. Anyway, he hasn't done that since Tracy was born, because he has more potential than that. That's why he's always inventing new ways to make his fortune.

He acts like this is going to be different from the firewood-cutting business that left us with no income in the summer. Then there were the booze bus, which not even a drunk person wanted to ride in, and the under-eighteen disco that no teen in their right mind would be seen at. And the metal detector on the beach that turned up nothing better than a broken watch and a fancy hair clip.

But this is it. This will change everything. No more getting up at three a.m. and dressing in his beige shorts and shirt to go to work at the courier company, delivering packages to people who don't even look you in the eye because to them you're not even there.

The next weekend Dad takes his machine out for a "suck and chuck," as he says.

He has the look of a man whose life is about to change.

When he comes back, he's covered in dirt and his boots are caked with mud, but he's got some little speckles in a jar. Mum's walking around the house furious, mumbling things under her breath like, "I'm fed up, Ron." He just wants us to have a better life. I don't know what's wrong with the one we have.

"You found gold—I knew you would, Dad!" I say, trying to be supportive.

"Only a little bit, love. These things take time. I've got to scan a lot of area before I can expect anything big," he says, sounding like he's not so sure.

He scans and scans for a couple of months, collecting a few more flecks before retiring his machine, "just for a while."

Money's tight, so Mum's going to work in an ice cream factory. Bad choice, if you ask me—too much temptation. She says she really wants to, that she's looking forward to sticking wooden sticks into ice creams as they roll past her on a conveyor belt. But I know better.

Except for Tracy, we all put on weight. It's hard to resist when you know there's a big freezer full of desserts in the kitchen. Mum's put on the most.

She quits right after Christmas, and Dad goes back to doing extra shifts at the courier company . . . at least until his next brainstorm.

I don't want to work in a factory. I'm destined for bigger things. I can feel it. I want to do more than just dream of doing things. I want an exciting life full of glamour and adventure.

Mum says that true actresses begin in the theater, so I've joined the Shopfront Theater for Young People. It really is a shopfront, a huge, brightly colored old house and store next to a railway line. There's an enormous theater, a room for screen printing, and a room for costumes. When I'm in the front office, I hear the trains outside. I imagine I'm in New York and Broadway is just around the corner.

I'm not overly religious or anything, but I pray every night. Now I have to pray even harder. Mum has a cyst in her stomach and I'm not sure how bad that is. For Mum. Can a cyst kill you?

I think about death a lot. It's Mum's fault, with all her talk about wanting to die first. Sometimes I wonder if it's that she cares so much about me or that she just doesn't want to go before me. She won't even let me walk home from school by myself, and no one I know has ever died walking home from school. Except once.

There was this little boy who was killed when some humongous paper rolls rolled right off the back of a truck and squashed him. I almost saw it. I'm glad I didn't. Some people like seeing that gory stuff, but not me.

It made all the mothers extra nervous, especially mine. Actually it made me nervous too . . . that you can die on the corner waiting for the lights to change.

"It's not a cyst."

"Well, what is it, then?" Tracy asks.

Mum's just come back from the doctor. She's standing at the kitchen sink, and I can't tell if she's going to laugh or cry.

"It's a baby," she says. "I'm going to have a baby."

I'm in shock. Mum and Dad still do it? Ewww. It

doesn't seem right. The last time they did it was probably when they had me.

"That's great, Mum," I say, hoping the disgust I feel doesn't show on my face. I'm excited at the prospect of a baby brother or sister, but how it came about, I don't want to know.

"Hey, Dad, it might be a boy. You'll have a son!" I say.

"Well, we'll see, hey," he says. I don't think he wants to get too excited in case he gets stuck with another girl in the house. First he hoped Tracy was a boy, then me, so I can sort of understand.

When I watch football with him, I think he can tell I'm not that interested. I just pretend to be. A son would probably care about the things Dad does, like fishing and sports and documentaries about tough men doing tough things like climbing mountains and diving for sunken treasure.

Mum's always been tired and unhealthy.

A few years ago, Dad forced Mum to go on a toboggan and she fell off and hurt her back. When checking to see if she was okay, the doctor found out she had kidney disease and had had it for a while. That explained her pale skin and the dark circles under her eyes and the fact that she's always so exhausted.

I suppose in a way Dad did Mum a favor. If Mum hadn't fallen off the toboggan, she would never have found out about her kidneys, and they might have gotten worse. Dad's always doing us "favors" like that. He always forces Tracy and me to do things we don't want to do. Like at the beach. We don't just relax on the sand and play in the surf. No, we do "activities," with Dad screaming at us the whole time.

It's a boy! Dad finally has a son.

Mum's beaming, and Tracy and I are finally off the hook. We have an adorable baby brother, and Dad now has a fishing, football, and general adventure partner.

His name is Trent. Mum and Dad liked John, but Tracy and I convinced them that he deserves a more distinctive name for when he grows up. So Trent John Vincent he is.

He's the cutest baby to ever have lived, and that's not just because I'm his sister. I've never seen a baby like this before. All soft and warm and gentle and cuddly with fine blond curls. He's even got Dad all gushy.

The baby will get my room; I'm moving to Tracy's room, which I'm excited about; and Tracy's getting our old living room (we added on a couple of years ago and have a bigger living room at the back of the house). She's graduating from school in a month and is about to start work as a hairdressing apprentice, so she plans to decorate her new room in a style befitting her new position in the world.

"It's going to be all designer white," she says.

Since Trent's arrival, Dad doesn't yell or throw things, and he smiles a lot more. And he doesn't stomp around with heavy feet and we don't have to walk on eggshells because of it. Probably because there's a baby in the house and he doesn't want to wake him. Whatever it is, I hope it lasts.

He's started singing a John Lennon song as Trent goes off to sleep. *"Close your eyes, have no fear . . . your daddy's here. Beautiful, beautiful, beautiful, beautiful boy."*

My dad's a big softie after all.

All my friends are going to a different high school. Because we live on the border of the school district, I'm stuck going to an all-girls' school with a reputation for drugs. I've heard that if you lift the drainage grates in the courtyard, you'll find syringes hanging there like ornaments on a Christmas tree. Apparently, this is the least of my problems. There's also the matter of pinning. Not the kind like the American movies from the fifties, where a girl wears a boy's pin to announce that they're dating, but the Australian kind, where you get a pin in your bum for being a new kid.

I'm in the assembly hall with all the other year seven girls—our first year of high school. There's a girl sitting next to me who doesn't look the least bit scared.

"Have you heard about the pinning?" I whisper to her as the principal drones on about what a great school community we're joining.

"Oh, I'm sure that's just a rumor," she whispers back. "I'm Julie."

We are given forms that tell us which class we're

going into: 7-1 is for the smartest, 7-6 is for the dumbest. Julie and I are in 7-2.

We walk to class together and quickly discover I was right and Julie was wrong. Pinning is alive and thriving at Beverly Hills Girls' High.

I feel a jab before I even get to first period. By second period, I'm walking with my back to the corridor walls.

"Erin, that's only going to make them notice you more," Julie laughs. She hasn't been pinned yet.

It went on for a few weeks. But I didn't care. I had a best friend.

My thirteenth birthday party.

Living on crackers, Tab, and Popsicles has paid off. I'm skinny. So I decide to have a pool party. For some reason, I'm nervous. I keep going to the bathroom. Suddenly I feel like something has just dropped inside of me and come out the other end. I stare into the toilet.

"Mum!" I yell. "I think my friends have arrived."

"There's no one here yet. They're not due till twelve o'clock."

"Not those friends, the other friends. You know, *friends* friends," I say in that "you know what I'm saying" voice.

Mum appears at the door. "Oh dear."

My stupid friends have come and they're not invited— some friends! No one told me it would be like this. It's not like cutting your finger or anything. This blood is all dark and lumpy and gooey.

How can I have a pool party like this?

"Calm down, Erin." My mother rummages under the bathroom sink. "Here, try this." She passes me a big fat maxi pad wrapped in pale pink plastic. Some birthday present!

"I can't put that mattress between my legs!"

"Just put it on," she says, trying to be sternly sweet.

I feel like I'm wearing one of Trent's diapers. "Mum, what am I going to do?"

Mum gets Tracy. "What is it? I'm going to be late," Tracy huffs. She's going out and hasn't finished blow-drying her hair.

"Erin's friends have just arrived," Mum whispers. "Maybe you could show her how to use a tampon so she can still go in the pool today?"

"Tampon? I'm not sticking one of those things up me!" I protest. "How will I know where to put it? What if I put it in the wrong hole?"

"It's not such a big deal, Erin," Tracy says, trying not to laugh. She shows me what to do. Tracy is being so nice about it, all helpful and sisterly. We finally have something in common: tampons.

I put it in the right hole. My real friends arrive. And the party starts.

I want a job. I want to be able to buy my own clothes and stuff. Mum says no one will hire me because I'm too young.

I decide to test this out. I spend a day walking from

store to store at the mall Tracy works at. I strike gold at Cookie Man. A peppy man with blond hair hands me a gingersnap and tells me I can fill out an application.

I walked to the back of the store and see the cookie-making machine churning dough and dropping dollops onto a metal tray before rolling them into the oven and popping them out the other end.

This is the place for me.

I'm afraid to tell the manager my age, but I'm also afraid of lying about it. So I tell him the truth. "I know I'm underage, but I'm a really hard worker," I confess hopefully.

It works. He asks me to come in next week and give it a try.

I've been asked to be part of the Shopfront Theater tour. Errol, Shopfront's founder, has chosen a cast of nine actors, ranging from ages eleven to twenty, to represent the theater by performing two plays in England, Scotland, and Wales next April, only ten months away.

"We're going to show the rest of the world just what kids can do," he says.

Now I just have to get Mum to let me go. She let me get a part-time job at Cookie Man in the mall. So . . .

"Please? I'm fourteen. This could be the start of something big."

But Mum isn't so sure. She shushes me each time I bring it up. "We'll think about it, Erin," she says, which usually translates into no.

But surprisingly, this time she says yes. She'll let me go off to England to die. That's what the decision is for her. That's how big it is. She isn't just letting me go to England on a six-week theater tour. In her mind she's letting me go off possibly never to come back—to die before her in some terrible accident. Maybe I get my dramatic nature from her.

I'm at Shopfront after a long day of rehearsal. Errol is yelling at us.

"Do you think we can take these plays overseas the way they are? We've been going over this for months now and it's still not good enough. You all have to work harder."

Errol yells and I love it, the drama of the theater. This is what it's all about.

I'm sitting on a dirty old green sofa with the foam popping out at the arms—very cool and artistic. Bright sunlight is coming in. Little specks of dust fly around, putting on their own little show. On the walls around me are photos of past productions and on the dirty red carpet are my bare bohemian feet.

My mind wanders. A daydream pops up out of nowhere.

I'll be sitting in this same chair a week from today and Mum and Dad will be gone. Tragedy will strike. Life will be ruined, changed forever. But the show must go on. I'll have to struggle on without them. I'll be up onstage rehearsing through the pain and everyone will think I'm noble and brave. Most people, if their parents died, would never be able to perform . . . but not me. I'm amazing and strong. It will be the best performance of my life. Everyone will say, *"Look at her! Isn't she incredible? A true star."*

I don't really mean it, God. Really, I don't. It's just some stupid scenario my fourteen-year-old brain came up with. It's the dramatic actress in me. Please don't listen to me, God. You wouldn't let anything like that happen. Of course you wouldn't.

October 23, 1983

I'm running.

And they chase me. I run down the stairs, around the first floor of the house, and back up again. I'm running nowhere, really, but I don't know what else to do.

They stop chasing me. They probably don't know what else to do either. My whole body is a scream. I want to run away from what I've just heard. I want to run out of myself, out of the nightmare, out of the thoughts in my head.

Then Uncle Steele catches me. His arms are strong. The house is spinning like Dorothy's in *The Wizard of Oz*. He hugs me and I think I'm going to be sick. Auntie

Connie, Theo, and Venise are crying and looking at me. None of us knows what to do.

"Come on, Erin." Auntie Connie is leading me to Venise's room. "Try and lie down."

I don't think I can. "What about Venise? Where will she sleep?" I feel sick.

Venise is standing in the doorway. "It's okay, Erin," she says.

Venise's room is all white and pink and pretty. Flowers everywhere, on the walls and on the bedspread I'm now lying under. I'm in a sea of flowers. I've stepped into a bad painting, like one of Mum's cheap production-line oils that Dad hates.

Every inch of me is shaking. Even my insides are shaking. I can't seem to control it. I'm shaking like Mum did when Nanny died. Does everyone shake this much when someone dies?

"I think we'd better call a doctor," Auntie Connie whispers to Uncle Steele.

Some time passes, but I don't know how much. A doctor arrives. He's old and gray and tall. He leans close to me. "I'm going to sedate you to calm you down and help you sleep."

"No, you're not!" I yell.

"It will help you," he tells me softly.

"Oh yeah?" My chin is trembling. "What, so I can go to sleep and wake up and have this start all over again? It'll be just as bad when I wake up."

He's not listening to me. He pulls a needle from his brown leather bag.

"No way. You're not sticking that needle in my arm." My voice is cold and determined.

So he doesn't. He leaves the room, followed by Uncle Steele.

I've got to stay awake. I've got to stay awake for when they finally find Tracy.

"Where is your sister?" Auntie Connie asks.

"Dancing," I say.

Tracy's a total disco freak. She wears tube tops and satin jeans that are so tight she has to lie on her bed to zip them up with a wire coat hanger. She looks amazing in them.

What will Tracy do? I don't want her to know. Mum's everything to her. Mum's her best friend. Tracy won't be able to take it. She's always dreamed of the good life. Nice clothes, nice car, dancing all night. She's the fun, popular party girl with a lot of living to do. This will ruin her.

I don't want her to feel this. I don't want to tell her, but I don't want anyone else to. I should be the one to do it. That seems like the right thing, the best thing.

There's a screech of tires outside.

They found her.

When Tracy walks through that door, life as she knows it will be over. She charges into the house and I'm out of bed with somewhere to go. I have to be the one to tell her.

"What's going on? What's all this crap about Mum?" she yells to no one in particular.

We're all standing in the living room near the front door.

I start to cry. "Tracy, there's been an accident. Mum's dead."

Just like that.

I've said it. Saying it out loud for the first time makes the horror suddenly seem even worse. Truer, somehow. I opened my mouth and out came the words I've always dreaded.

"That's ridiculous!" Tracy's laughing. "Where is she?"

"She's dead, Tracy. She's dead. Please believe me," I beg, crying. "They went to Liverpool Hospital. Tracy, Mum's dead," I blubber.

Now she's really angry.

"Liverpool Hospital? This is stupid, Erin. I'm going to the hospital to find Mum."

"Can I come?"

"Stay here!"

"Please!" I'm still crying.

"No." She seems mad at me. Like it's my fault, like I made it happen and have no right to go with her.

"Tracy, let me drive you," Uncle Steele says.

"No. I'm fine," she says, all composed.

She storms out. The shaking is starting again. "Here, Erin, wrap this blanket around you," Auntie Connie says, trying not to cry.

The pale blue blanket is soft and warm.

I suppose I did make it happen for Tracy. I'm the one who told her.

Tracy's back. Her face looks empty. Mum's dead and she knows it.

I don't know what to do. I don't know what to say. I don't even know what I'm feeling. This can't be happening. I'm going to wake up soon and I'll be back home in my bed. Dad will be up, whistling to the radio as he makes breakfast. Tracy will be sleeping in, and Mum will be getting dressed while Trent stands next to her chatting away in his husky little voice.

"We've got to get Trent. He's still at Evelyn's," I say, crying.

Although Evelyn is Mum's best friend and I know he's safe, I want Trent. We've got to get Trent. What are we going to do about Trent? What's he going to do? I want Trent.

It's now four o'clock in the morning. Everyone's talking so low.

"I guess we better go home," Tracy says. I'm staring at one of Auntie Connie's tapestries on the wall. I guess there's no point in finishing mine now.

"You can stay for as long as you want, you know," Uncle Steele says.

"No, we really should go," Tracy says, determined.

"We're here if you need us," Auntie Connie says, hugging me.

"Thanks, Auntie Connie," I say, unwrapping myself from the blanket.

"No, Erin. Keep it."

Tracy and I are standing at the top of the hill. The same hill we used to skateboard down.

I don't want to go home, but Tracy says we have to.

I'm walking wrapped in a blanket like those people in old movies on their way to the gallows. They know what's in store for them, but they don't *really* know. It's misty and quiet. I can almost hear the drum beating in the background. No, that's my heart. There I go again. Why am I always so melodramatic?

We're here. Our little redbrick house at the bottom of the cul-de-sac. I don't want to go in there. I can't.

"Do you have your keys?" Tracy asks.

"Yes," I say, but I can't find them. This makes her mad, so I find them.

I knew it would all be different when we came back. I knew when I locked that door that I was shutting it all away.

We walk in.

Everything is different.

I go straight to my bedroom and scream into my pillow.

October 24, 1983

Tracy's boyfriend, Chris, arrives in the early morning. She must have called him.

Tracy was scared to introduce him to Dad. She knew Dad would be furious when he found out her boyfriend had sun-bleached long hair and wore tie-dyed T-shirts and rode a motorcycle. But finally she did it, and now Chris is almost like one of the family. He went fishing with Dad a few times and they really bonded. Dad even bought him a radio for Christmas.

Mum loved Chris instantly. "He's a gentle soul," she said.

We walk outside, get in the car, and drive to the hospital to see Dad. For once I don't want food.

It's a long drive, at least an hour. Why couldn't they have been run over in a nicer, cleaner suburb closer to home? What am I thinking? Why do I care?

Chris is driving Tracy's hotted-up bright red VW Beetle. I wonder if anyone else out there in one of those cars is feeling what we're feeling. I wonder if we've passed someone on their way to the hospital to visit their dad after their mum has just died. I feel numb.

There's not much to say when we see Dad. He's groggy and just cries and says he's sorry before falling asleep. So we stand and watch him. He's in intensive care. It's all white and sterile but noisy and messy, like there's too much crammed into one big room. There are machines and cords everywhere. Most of the people in the beds look like they are fighting to stay alive.

Dad's got tubes everywhere. Circular white electrical pads are stuck to his chest. He's as white as the brightly lit room, with dried purple blood on his head that they haven't washed off yet. When I lean in close, I notice that Dad smells like a hospital, where everything's decaying but covered up with cleaning fluids.

All of a sudden there's a code blue or red or whatever and we're told to go outside while they deal with the man next to Dad. We stand out in the waiting room with all the not-so-urgent bloody, messy people waiting to be seen by a doctor.

When we're allowed back in, we talk to the nurses. I wonder if any of them is the bitch who hung up on me last night. These nurses do seem nice, though. Maybe they're just rude when they can't see your face. I can tell they feel really bad for Dad. They fuss over him and seem genuinely concerned. Besides the fact that his legs are completely crushed, I think they know his wife just died. But he's alive and out of danger, they say.

He may be in a wheelchair for a very long time, but "He's not going to die, Erin," a nice nurse tells me after I ask her for the tenth time.

Dad's not going to be awake for a while, so we decide to go and pick up Trent from Auntie Evelyn's.

As we start to walk out, we hear yelling down the corridor. "Where's Ronnie? Where's our Ronnie?" It's Grandma and Grandpa–Dad's parents.

"He's asleep," I tell them, and they push me out of the way and keep walking.

On the drive to Evelyn's, Tracy tells us what happened.

"Last night Dad told me they were crossing the road to go to a fruit stand when a speeding tow truck came out of nowhere and hit them," she says staring straight ahead.

We drive in silence.

As soon as we see Trent, everything seems worse. He's delicate and small. He turned three only a week ago. Hopefully he's too young to completely understand what's going on.

Evelyn looks how we feel. Like someone's jumped out of nowhere and punched her in the face.

"Oh God, oh God" is all she manages to mutter before we leave.

At first we don't say anything to Trent. We wait for him to ask, which he does when we get to the car.

"Where's Mummy and Daddy?"

I'm trying not to cry, and I think Tracy and Chris are too.

"Mummy's not here," Tracy tells him.

After a long pause I say, "She's gone . . . um . . . gone to heaven," not knowing if it's the right thing or if I'm screwing him up for life.

"Oh. When is she coming back?" he asks.

"Oh, Trent, Mummy loves you so much, but when you go to heaven, you stay there with God," Tracy says with tears streaming down her face.

He looks at us without saying anything. For the rest of the trip I pretend things are normal. I ask all about what he did at Evelyn's. I even laugh at something.

"Do you think he understands?" I ask Chris later, when Trent has fallen asleep in his car seat.

"No, I doubt it," he says, as unsure as I am.

I wonder if Trent's little heart, probably the size of a golf ball, feels it. What does he feel?

As soon as we're home, the phone starts ringing. One of the first calls is from Ronald and Peter—Mum's younger brothers. Although they're my uncles, I've never called them that. They're too young and cool. They're coming here with their wives, Gai and Frances. They live out where Nanny's grave is. The grave Mum and Dad were visiting only yesterday.

Before they get here, I start wondering. Do I buy them something to cheer them up? Do I give them a sympathy card or flowers? Does one griever do something like that for another griever? Peter did that for me when Nanny died. Even though Nanny was *his* mother and only my grandmother, Peter went out and bought presents for both Tracy and me. He said he wanted to cheer us up, and he did. I got a hardcover Muppet Show book, which I read from cover to cover, over and over again, and Tracy got the Rod Stewart album *Blondes Have More Fun*. I couldn't believe that Peter would think of us when he himself was in mourning. He's amazing.

Peter's always joking. Whenever he comes over for dinner, he does everything he can to drive Mum crazy. He taught me how to flick peas with a spoon so they'd land wherever I wanted. He teases Mum over her obsession with her crystal and china and fancy dining room set.

"Oh no, Bev, I've spilt gravy on the velvet!" he says, his eyes twinkling.

Mum loves her "baby" brothers, even though they're grown-ups now. She thinks they're two of the best people on earth.

Why am I talking about Mum like she's still here?

Peter's wife, Frances, is from Holland. She's long and lanky and Mum calls her Frankie, which makes her feel special. She loves Mum. With her strawberry-blond hair and tiny freckles, she's the poster girl for clogs and wind-mills. She and Peter are a really cute couple.

Ronald and Gai look kind of strange together. Almost like brother and sister. They both have the same short brown frizzy hair, like steel wool. (Ronald even has it on his back, which I try my best not to look at.) Ronald's a lot like Dad in the humor department. He's always up to mischief. In every family photo Ronald is giving Mum rabbit's ears. Gai is short and serious, like a bulldog. Humor isn't really her thing, but I like her okay.

So anyway, they're all here and it feels kind of nice.

We get sent lots of ugly flowers. The kind you only send to dead people because no one living should have to look at such crap. The house is full of unattractive carna-tions. Vases of flowers line Dad's bar (he would not be thrilled to know this).

Hello! Don't forget for one minute why we're here. We're the flowers that say your mum's dead. Remember?

They're laughing at me.

I'm living in a funeral home.

We're all walking around the house without a pur-pose. Trent walks from room to room like he's looking for something. He doesn't say what. But we know.

It's all a blur. One day blends into another.

People have been to visit, but I don't remember who, except for Auntie Connie and the other neighbors. Auntie Connie comes every day with a casserole or roast. Venise comes with her sometimes, but right now there's nothing regular to talk about, so seeing her feels weird.

"You've got to eat and keep up your strength," Auntie Connie tells us.

"Thanks, Auntie Connie, we will. Thank you so much," Tracy says each time.

We end up with a freezer full of casseroles.

I love Auntie Connie's Greek food and am shocked that I don't want to eat it. Other people who visit are hungry, though, and thanks to her, we don't have to cook.

I walk around the house with my head down. I've never noticed before how ugly our carpet is. It looks like squares of green puke. Imagine eating a meal of spinach, peas, and beans. Now follow this up with some yummy green jelly with mint ice cream on top. You've eaten yourself silly, so silly that you're sick all over the floor. Look down—that's what our carpet looks like.

I feel like my head is blocked. It's like someone has turned the sound down. It's that sound when you're underwater in the pool and the voices above the water are muffled and the clearest thing you can hear is your heartbeat. Mine is louder than anything else, until the phone rings.

That phone won't stop ringing. I want to pull it out of the wall. I should have that night—no phone, no news. Leave us alone, but don't leave us alone. Tracy looks at me, knowing it's her turn to answer it. We've each spoken to at least ten people today and it's only lunchtime.

"Oh, hello. . . . Yes, I know. . . . Okay. Thanks. . . .

Thank you. That means a lot. . . . Okay, bye." Tracy delivers her monologue into the receiver. I know what the person on the other end is saying, because they all say a version of the same thing:

"Hi, Erin. Oh it's awful, just awful. How are you and Tracy holding up? If you need anything, anything"—(they say things twice for effect)—*"please just call. We're here for you. Well, we'll speak to you soon. Don't forget to call if you need us. Bye now."*

"Can't we just disconnect it for a while?" I ask.

"No, we might miss a call from the hospital," Tracy says, as if that should be obvious.

"Oh yeah, I didn't consider that," I say. I feel like a thoughtless brat.

The house is slightly more bearable with family staying here. It's not so quiet and still and dark and cold. There are even moments of laughter when we talk about Mum. I hope that's not wrong. I hope God doesn't punish us.

Gai and Frances are trying to encourage Tracy and me to eat by saying "Think of Trent," but we know Trent will be all right as long as *he* eats. Tonight they've heated up two of Auntie Connie's casseroles and have set the table. They've put Mum's favorite tablecloth with the big English flowers on the table, and her special crystal glasses have been taken from the cabinet. It doesn't feel right for us all to eat at Mum's dining table without her.

We make a toast "to Beverly." Why do they call it a toast when Mum's now toast?

I want to be sick but there's nothing in my stomach to bring up. So I cry instead.

"I'm sorry, I'm sorry," I blubber.

"Oh, Erin, it's okay. We all feel like crying," Frances says, getting up to hug me.

I want her to and I don't want her to. I'm strange the past two days. I feel like I want someone to hug me, and then when they do, it repulses me. I gently wriggle out of her hug, pretending I need to get a tissue.

I feel guilty knowing Dad's in the hospital tonight being spoon-fed mush from a plastic TV tray. No wonder I can't eat! When we visited him this afternoon, there was a plate by his bed with nothing eaten off it. That's not like Dad. Maybe if he were here with us, he'd eat something.

Everyone's impressed with Auntie Connie's cooking. Even Trent's eating, and he's been Mr. Fussy lately. I move my food around on my plate and put my fork to my mouth every now and again for effect. Tracy doesn't even bother pretending, and we all know by now not to mention it. If she hardly eats when life is normal, there's no way she's going to eat now.

October 26, 1983

Mum's been gone for three days, and it's Tracy's eighteenth birthday. I'm not sure what to say to her. A happy birthday it is not.

"Tracy, it's your birthday today," I say quietly.

"Thanks for reminding me, Erin," she snaps.

Peter and Ronald ask Chris what we should do for her birthday, and Chris says we should just keep quiet about it.

Tracy had big plans. She was going to go out with Chris and all their friends. I wonder if she'll ever want to do that again.

October 28, 1983

Tracy won't let me help her organize Mum's funeral.
She's sitting at the table with stacks of papers from the funeral home. It doesn't seem right that she should do this
alone, but she won't have it any other way.

"I don't need your help with this, Erin. I'm the one
who knows best what she would want."

"But I want to help," I tell her, sitting down and picking up a glossy pamphlet about coffins. Apparently, there
are lots to choose from.

"I'm fine!" she says, snatching the pamphlet back.
"Just forget it."

An eighteen-year-old daughter shouldn't have to do

this for her forty-one-year-old mother, but I suppose in a way Tracy's not really a teenager anymore.

"Will you at least let Ronald and Peter look at this stuff when they get home from food shopping?" I ask.

"Okay. All right. Now stop being such a pain and let me do this," she says, getting annoyed.

So I go into my room and think about flowers, then coffins, then dead bodies, then dead bodies covered in dirt, then skeletons, then maggots.

I wish she'd just let me look at the pamphlets.

October 30, 1983

It's a week since the accident and I'm going back to school.

I'm going back to school because I don't know what else to do.

I'm going back to school because I don't want to be here.

I'm going back to school because everyone says I should.

I'm going back to school because I have to put one foot in front of the other.

I'm going back to school because I'm noble and wise. I'm strong. I'm to be admired.

"Look, she's going back to school! How very brave of her!" they'll all say.

I'm going back to school because sooner or later I have to. I have to prove to myself that my life isn't over, that I have a choice. If I don't go back to school, I'll fall so far behind I'll never catch up, and life will never get better. I'll forever be the girl without a mother. It will ruin everything.

I'm going back to school and I have no real reason why.

I'm going back to school and I didn't sleep a wink. Every time I try to close my eyes, I see rotting flesh and skeletons and Mum lying in the middle of the road. It's so overpowering. Why can't I get this out of my mind? I didn't sleep and I look like shit. In a way I'm secretly pleased. I know it's wrong, but I can't help it. The black circles under my red eyes are a great effect. If I went to school looking too good, they'd think I was over it, just like the movies. They'd think I was over it and expect too much of me. I don't even know what to expect.

I don't know how the hell I'm going to cope in front of everyone.

I hope not too many people know.

It's weird putting on my ugly traffic-light green school uniform for the first time since it all happened. It feels loose and baggy. I would've killed for that before. Why did it take a tragedy for me to lose weight? I put my shoes on and they feel like someone else's. I put another girl's books in another girl's bag. Brush my limp blond hair that looks thinner than ever before. I didn't think that was possible. I'm disappearing before my very eyes. Am I really here? Is this all really happening?

Get moving, that's the trick. Got to keep busy.

Now all I have to do is walk up our little hill, get on the bus, get off the bus and walk up the long, long hill to school.

> *When we come, when we come*
> *To the school on the hill*
> *Proudly we come with our hearts and our*
>   *hopes held high*
> *With a faith that is strong we blah blah blah*
>   *blah blah blah blahhhhhhhhh.*

I always fake it from there because I'm not sure of the words. A school song is like a national anthem. You're supposed to know the words. I've always thought our school song was dumb. Singing it to the tune of that Elvis song "Wooden Heart" doesn't help things either.

I'll never forget the day Elvis died. I hardly knew who he was. He was just some handsome, shiny-black-haired man who seemed to spend all his time singing and kissing girls in Hawaii. Anyway, there I was standing in line outside in the heat waiting to go into my third-grade class when a teary-eyed teacher came out and said Elvis had just died. I stood there and cried. I'll never know why I cried for Elvis. Maybe because Dad looks a bit like him—the fat seventies Elvis, that is.

And here I am years later crying again and thinking about that stupid school song and actually buying into what it says. I must really be losing my mind, finding meaning in our school song. What a nerd! Secretly, though, I am trying to hold my heart up, and I do have high hopes and all that bullshit. I suppose I just keep thinking that if I get back into my normal routine, all this will be over.

I have to say goodbye to Trent. I don't want to leave him. What if I go to school and he thinks I'm never coming back? What if something happens to him while I'm gone? I get this feeling that as long as I keep my eyes on him, he'll be all right. I'll be there to make sure nothing bad happens to him. Maybe I could take him with me for show-and-tell. My own walking, talking cherub-faced doll.

Peter tells me he'll drive me to school. I don't have to walk up that hill. I don't think I could do that today.

When I walk through the metal front gate, my school looks bigger than I remember it. The eucalyptus trees surrounding it look taller. I feel smaller.

I walk inside to go find Julie. We spoke last night on the phone and decided to meet by our lockers.

Everyone is looking at me. I can feel it. They're averting their eyes, but they're looking. Maybe death sticks to you.

Do they all know? How could they?

They'd better not know. I don't want them to feel sorry for me.

I imagine people whispering. *"There's the girl whose mother just died. She was hit by a tow truck!"*

I keep walking down the hall. I wonder if they're thinking, *Look at her. She's a freak.*

Finally, I spot Julie.

"I don't know if I can do this," I whisper.

"Let's just stick together all day. And if it gets too bad you can always leave," she says with a sad smile.

I catch a glimpse of the stupid Christians. We have quite a few of them at school. I can just imagine what they're saying in their lunchtime God group. *"We should pray for her. That'll help."* Fuck off, you morons. It's too late. I already asked. There is no God. Actually, I don't know what I believe anymore.

It's amazing how when people are trying hard not to look at you, that's when you feel them looking at you the most. I feel like a minicelebrity, a celebrity of the tragic, suffering kind. Drama, not comedy. Although sometimes it feels like a joke. Is this how famous people feel? I've always dreamed of standing in the spotlight, but this isn't quite the stardom I was searching for.

And the award for best performance in a suburban tragedy goes to . . . Erin Vincent! Wild applause, possibly a standing ovation.

I'd like to thank my parents for obvious reasons (a little ironic laughter there); my supporting cast of mourners,

I couldn't have done it without you; and . . . (a bit choked up here) and above all I'd like to thank God, my creator, for making all this possible! Oh yeah, and I should dedicate the award to Mum, that's always a tearjerker. Oh, and I shouldn't forget a tear or two myself. Noble, stoic tears, of course.

Here comes Mrs. C-J, my religious studies teacher, bounding down the corridor. She's got on her big smiley smile and her elastic-waist jeans. Why do Christians have no sense of style? Does she ever *not* smile? It must be a lot of pressure to have to look like you're basking in the Lord's glory all the time. Religious studies is actually one of my favorite classes. I always catch her out with something God got wrong. There's always a question that stumps her. When that happens, she says, "Oh, that's God's will."

I'd like to read God's will sometime.

"Hi, Erin, we're so glad you're back with us. How are you?"

"Oh, just peachy keen. What do you think?" I want to say.

"Good, thanks," I say.

All of sudden I want her to hug me even though she's always annoyed me with her goody-goodiness. What a pathetic, needy wimp I've become!

"Now, I want you to know that everybody cares and is here for you. We've all been praying for you, Erin. All of us, the whole school. We had a special prayer in assembly on Monday."

"What? You mean everyone knows?"

"Yes, Erin. There's nothing wrong with people knowing."

Oh great, now they'll all think I'm pathetic. I'm so angry. No, I'm fucking furious. How dare she! The absolutely most important thing for me is that no one know so they don't pity me, and she's taken that away without even asking.

"Who told everyone?" I ask angrily.

"Erin, it's been on the news."

I want to scream, but like a big fat sucker who's all "boo hoo" and no "fuck you," I just smile and say, "Thanks for praying, Mrs. C-J, that's really nice and thoughtful. I do feel funny that everybody knows, though."

"Erin, we *care*. There's no shame in people knowing," she says, secure in the knowledge that she's done an incredibly good deed for a motherless child and now has a higher seat in the staff room of heaven. Well, that's what she thinks! What about what I think? Is that irrelevant now? Do I have no say in anything from now on? It's still my life, isn't it? I should get to choose who knows what. Keeping it to myself was the one thing I thought I had control over. The one thing I thought was mine.

"But I really didn't *want* anyone to know," I say. "They'll all just feel sorry for me."

She'd better *not* try to hug me.

I hate her for making it such a big deal. I hate her for butting in where's she's not wanted, yet I don't know how I'd feel if she didn't. It shows she cares, I suppose. Although, she is the religion teacher, and Christians are supposed to care—it's in their job description. Maybe she's just doing her duty.

"I've got to get to class," I say, and storm off for effect.

I can do that now, walk away from a teacher in a huff. They'll be too scared to say anything. It's like I've been given a special license. I wonder when it expires?

I'm in my homeroom and I want to cry, but I won't.

The room seems much bigger than before, and there's nowhere to hide. I stare at the walls. Deep breaths, Erin, deep breaths. You can do this. Prove that you're stronger than most people would be in your position. Prove that you're someone special.

I look around. Homeroom is full of girls from every grade. It's a new thing they're trying, to see if we can all bond and become a better school community. We sit in silence for fifteen minutes every morning and read whatever we want. I love the reading part, but I don't think we'll all bond this way, with our heads in books. I'm reading *Flowers in the Attic*. I love it. It's about three children with a mean mother who locks them in an attic. Why don't *those* kinds of mothers die?

I have now read the same sentence three times. Concentrate. Concentrate. Are people looking at me? Concentrate, for God's sake. Not that I'd do anything right now for *God's* sake. He can get lost.

Math. My worst subject and teacher. What a fabulous start to a simply marvelous day!

Mrs. Pike doesn't seem so bad today. She's usually so official and uptight, like she has a protractor up her butt, but today she's almost smiling. The muscles in her face are actually moving. Even her straight brown hair looks different, long and loose instead of glued to the top of her head in a bun. She almost looks human.

"Welcome back, Erin."

I don't believe it. She spoke to me like I'm a real person, not just a brain with numbers waiting to be added and subtracted. See what your mother's dying gets you?

There's a group of six of us friends who sit together at lunch: me, Megan the ballerina, Lorraine the runner, Linda the netball player, Meredith the activist, and Julie. Julie and I like to act stupid at every opportunity. It makes school more interesting. Her nickname is Speck. I don't know how it started except to say she looks like a tiny speck. She's even shorter than me, which is saying something. She's as skinny as can be, with a face that's round and square at the same time, and her short brown hair has curls that go every which way. Her forehead's so high you could write a story on it.

Julie's the smartest person I know. I walk away from a situation thinking of all the things I could have said, but not Julie. She walks away relishing the things she *did* say. She's quick and she makes me laugh, which I think I'll be needing a lot of now. She's probably the reason I can even think of getting through today.

I'm walking with my friends along the beige corridors, on the beige linoleum floor, from class to class. I'm in a daze and don't really hear anything the teachers say. I just copy down what they write on the blackboard and keep to myself. Except in science. My teacher, Mrs. Stockbridge, welcomes me back with a hug and gives me a warm smile. She makes everything seem like it might be manageable.

I try not to think bad thoughts. I absolutely must not cry. I don't want people to think I'm weak. But I am. I cry in economics and geography. I hate these subjects, so maybe that has something to do with it. Who cares about money and rocks at a time like this?

Tracy and Trent are picking me up from school so we can drive straight to the hospital to see Dad.

The VW Beetle is in the school parking lot and everyone looks at it, not because it's the grief girl's car but because it's so cool you can't *not* look at it. I feel proud to walk toward it. It's like saying, "Yeah, my mother's dead, but I'm no loser."

I didn't really notice this before, but the hospital Dad is in is like a five-star hotel.

When we walk in, I try to pretend I actually *am* in a five-star hotel.

I'm waltzing down the rust-colored carpeted corridor. I'm not in a hospital. I'm off to my penthouse suite— although the smell makes the lie more difficult to believe.

And then I see Dad. He looks disgusting. Not like a hotel guest in a plush bathrobe. Sure, he's now in a room by himself, but he's wearing a paper hospital gown. His crushed legs are under a blanket. I don't know why they leave that caked-on blood around his head. It looks like the almost-black red color of my nails. I decide to change my nail polish as soon as I get home.

Lies we tell Dad:

"You look so much better today."

"We're doing great."

"Don't worry about Trent. He's fine."

"Oh, I'm back at school and it's going really well, actually."

I wonder what happens to Dad when we're not around. What does he go through? He never lets us know.

One nurse told us he cries all day. She said he cries hardest in the bathroom. The nurse knows because she has to take him there. He can't move his legs. Apparently, when he's sitting on the special seat in the shower, she can hear his sobs over the sound of the rushing water. I don't know why she thought we needed to know this.

Dad feels so guilty.

"I'm sorry, I'm so sorry," he sobs over and over again. "It's all my fault. She didn't want to cross the road. She didn't want to go to the fruit stand. She said, 'No, Ron, let's just get home.' But I got angry and made her."

I'm not going to cry even though my eyes are getting that hot feeling. I've got to be positive for Dad.

"You have nothing to be sorry for, Dad," I say, but he won't stop crying and apologizing.

He doesn't realize yet that the accident was my fault. I made it happen by thinking it. I only wish I had the courage to tell him.

This isn't the first time I've been guilty of killing something.

I killed the pet mouse Julie gave me for my fourteenth birthday.

I forgot to feed it and it died. I was a teenage murderer! Or, if it wasn't on purpose, is it manslaughter? Or should I say *mouse*-slaughter. No, it was outright murder, no matter how I looked at it.

It wouldn't have happened if he'd gotten a bit of cheese every once in a while. But no, I was too busy to think of that. How could I have been so cruel and selfish?

For days after he died, every time I closed my eyes I imagined that little mouse crawling around desperate for food . . . every day getting weaker and weaker. Oh, how he must have suffered! What a slow and painful death it must have been . . . and it was going on right in my bedroom! He was dying right before my very eyes—if I'd bothered to look!

I decided I should be made to suffer the way he suffered. I took my punishment into my own hands. I will feel what he felt, I determined; I will feel hunger and thirst and pain. I will become the mouse.

I vowed that from that moment on, no food or drink would pass my lips. If he endured it, then so would I. I had to be made to suffer. It was the only way.

So the next day I got up and went to school without breakfast.

By the time I got there I was dreaming of Big Macs and French fries, but there was no way I was going to give in.

I had to suffer.

"Why aren't you eating?" Julie asked, as I knew she would. She cares. She's not the kind of person who would starve anything.

"Oh, I don't feel so great," I said. And it was true. I didn't. I couldn't hold out any longer. I got a milk shake. It's a drink, I told myself. Not food.

I lasted two days on milk shakes alone before giving up. I lied to Julie. I couldn't tell her the truth. Instead, I told her the mouse died from some unknown cause.

"I don't know," I said, "one minute he was okay and the next time I looked he was dead."

I should be dead instead.

November 1, 1983

Mrs. C-J thinks I should go and look at Mum's body. She hasn't been buried yet because they have to do an autopsy. I can't bear to think of them cutting her open.

"It will help you believe it," Mrs. C-J says. "You'll be better able to accept it." Maybe she's right. Maybe I should see Mum's body. I can't seem to grasp that my mother is dead, that her body has no life in it anymore, that she'll never be walking and talking again. She'll never hug me again. Why can't I believe it? I haven't seen her for almost two weeks, and that's never happened. I can't call her on the phone, I can't write her a letter and expect one in return. She's gone and I know it, but at the same time I don't. I can't get my head around it.

Maybe seeing her lying there in a coffin would make it real. But would she be in a coffin yet or on one of those cold metal drawers they pull out of the fridge at the morgue? If I see it, will that be my last memory of her? Will that be all I remember because I'll be so traumatized I won't be able to think of anything else? I'll try to see that rare smile of hers or her small, quiet eyes, and all I'll see is a cold, closed mouth and closed eyes with nothing but death and pain behind them. They said she died instantly and felt no pain. I love that. How do they know? Have they ever died instantly? And did she really die instantly, or is that just something they tell the poor grieving children to comfort them?

"Oh, Erin, that's sick! God, you're melodramatic!" Tracy said when I asked what she thought about going to the morgue.

I'm not going to go. I don't want the nightmares Tracy says I'll have.

I can't even think of Mum in that place.

If only . . .
I could turn back the clock.
I could go back and stop them leaving home that
    Sunday.
They had gone to visit Nanny's grave the day before.
Mum had stayed in the car.
Dad weren't so forceful.
They had crossed the road two seconds later or two
    seconds earlier.

They had crossed a little faster or a little slower.

There had been a crosswalk.

They hadn't been holding hands.

The fruit stand had been closed.

They had kept driving.

The car wouldn't start when they left the cemetery.

They had wasted a few minutes calling me before they
left.

The tow truck hadn't been speeding.

The truck had hit them differently.

I had been with them.

I had been a better daughter.

I hadn't thought that thought.

This were a dream.

They say they can fix Dad. Rebuild him. Better, faster,
stronger than he was before.

The world's first bionic dad.

Ron Vincent will be that dad.

They're going to put metal pins that look like big fat
skewers into his legs.

I work myself up to be happy and bright when I
see him. I want to joke about Dad Kebabs, Roasted Ron,
Fondue Father, Pierced Parent, Barbecued Big Daddy,
but maybe now's not the time to try and cheer him up the
old faithful way. Usually you can cheer Dad up with a
joke. Not anymore. Dad's legs are crushed. The doctors
say the pins might never help, but they've got to give it
a try.

"There is a possibility that he'll be in a wheelchair for the rest of his life," the doctor says.

"No, that's not right," I want to say. *"This is my big hearty dad you're talking about. You don't know him. He just won't stand for that. I mean he* will *stand. That's my whole point."*

"Anything is possible. We just have to wait and see. Now he's in a lot of pain, so he might not be able to talk long," the doctor says on his way out. My dad is just one in a long line of patients to him.

It's late, so we have to leave too. This is the worst part. We lift Trent up to kiss Dad goodbye before the three of us walk out and leave him there all alone.

At least Tracy, Trent, and I have each other.

I don't feel so alone at school anymore.

I have my friends, but I can't burden them with my problems all the time. Julie's been great. She treats me the same as she always has and listens to me go on and on about how terrible I feel. But I don't want her to get sick of me.

"If you ever need someone to talk to, Erin, I'm here," my science teacher, Mrs. Stockbridge, told me the other day.

I want so badly to do well in science, so I'm going to study extra hard. Mrs. Stockbridge isn't like the other teachers. She just looks me in the eye and comes right out and says it.

"I can't even begin to imagine how you must feel, Erin. It's just devastating."

She doesn't tell me she knows how I feel or that "time heals all wounds."

She doesn't say "Just give it time," like all the other adults do, because she knows that time is the problem. Everything moves so slowly. The time it's going to take to get through this is what scares me. Don't talk to me about time!

I now spend almost every lunch period with Mrs. Stockbridge. It's the only way I can get through the day. We sit in her classroom at a gray lab table by the Bunsen burners and eat our sandwiches and talk. She hasn't said why, but I can see that she finds life hard too.

It's the day of Dad's surgery and all I can think of is the game Operation.

I keep seeing Dad's nose buzz bright red whenever they touch his skin with their metal instruments. I can't get the image out of my head.

I wish Dad's only problem were a charley horse (a white plastic horse) or water on the knee (a little plastic bucket). But this isn't a game.

Tracy and I are in the waiting room. Trent is at home with Ronald, Peter, Gai, and Frances. We sit and stare straight ahead at the reproduction modern art on the walls until Dad's parents arrive. I hate when they come to the hospital; they're so dramatic it's sickening.

"What's happening to our Ronnie?" Grandma shrieks while Grandpa walks behind her picking his nose. Grief sure doesn't stop some people from being their annoying selves.

"Stop yelling, for God's sake! He's being operated on now," Tracy says.

Grandma frowns. "I've got to talk to someone about this." And with that, my grandparents walk toward the nursing station.

Tracy and I look at each other and roll our eyes. All they do is make every situation more tense. But at least hating them gives Tracy and me something to bond over.

"He will come out? He won't die in there, will he?" I ask the doctor when he comes to see us. He's dressed in scrubs and ready to operate.

He smiles. "Don't worry. We do this kind of surgery all the time."

I believe him when he says it's a common operation, but death's common too. People can die when you least expect it. But I can't think like that. I've got to stay positive. I can't have bad thoughts. Bad thoughts make bad things happen.

Stay happy.

When we see Dad hours later, he doesn't seem to be in much pain. He just looks sleepy. It probably helps that Dad's always been really big and strong. I have to admit, though, he doesn't look very strong right now with his white hospital gown and bedpan under the bed. I wonder if he's hiding the pain or if the sadness just numbs everything else.

"How are you feeling, Dad?" I whisper. Why am I whispering? It's weird, but I feel like if I talk loud, my voice will reverberate through the air and the sound waves will hurt his legs.

Sometimes when we visit Dad we just make small talk, which seems really stupid. But you can't talk about death and crushed legs and stuff all the time. Trent helps. He keeps our minds off why we're here. We watch him run around the room, sit "very still, now" on Dad's bed, and just generally act like his cute three-year-old self.

He reminds us all to be strong.

Mum's funeral is today and Dad can't go. He's begged the doctors to put him on a stretcher and take him there in an ambulance, but they say he can't be moved. So Dad has to just lie there in the hospital while his wife's funeral takes place. That can't be good for his mental health. Mrs. C-J told me that a funeral is necessary to help you accept that someone has died. How will Dad accept it? I suppose he saw Mum's body lying there on the road, so maybe that's enough for him to know she's dead for sure.

It's weird getting dressed for your mother's funeral.

It's almost like dressing for a party. Then you notice the silence all around you. There's no laughing. No music playing. No mother to call from another room to see how you're doing. Then you remember what you're really dressing for.

You're putting on a pink dress to bury your mother.

It was Mum's favorite, and I'll be damned if I'll wear depressing old black! I'm not some sheep who follows the flock . . . although right now I kind of feel like the black sheep. No one thinks I'm old enough to know all the details of today.

I'm dressed and ready. I look in the mirror.

It's amazing how good I look. I should look terrible and grief stricken, but I don't. I look so wonderful, people will probably think I didn't really love my mother and this is just another day in the park for me.

Peter comes in. "The cars are here. It's time to leave." He's been speaking in a hushed tone all morning. They all have. It's driving me crazy and making everything seem worse. It's not like Mum's hovering above us listening. That stuff's for people who need something to believe in.

I don't want to go. I'm in a pink dress and I'm going to my mother's funeral. I look in the mirror again and tell myself to stop being such a wimp.

I still look wonderful.

I go outside into the blaring sun. It's so hot the pebbles on the verandah look like they're boiling.

Tracy is in the street, stepping into one of the shiny black cars with Chris. She didn't want to sit with me. Probably worried I'd be a big crybaby. I think I'm getting on her nerves.

I walk toward the car behind hers. I feel like I'm going to be sick. This kind of car doesn't belong in our happy little cul-de-sac. A fat man in a black suit gives me that

"I'm so sorry" smile and opens the back door for me. I feel like a movie star going to the Academy Awards.

I'm so shallow.

It's terrible that Dad can't be here.

Trent is digging in a sandbox at a neighbor's house while our mother is being buried. How bloody ironic!

I get my own shiny black luxury funeral car all to myself. I feel so grown-up all of a sudden. I suppose if there's a time to stop being a kid, this is it. It's so quiet out here. It's as though all the birds and trees know we're going to a funeral. How can they know? How is it that it's so quiet?

Frances taps on the window. "Can I ride with you?"

I know she's only doing it for my sake, and I do kind of like the idea of traveling by myself, but maybe it's for the best.

"Okay, that might be good," I tell her.

We're off.

The car is going very slowly. Why are they dragging this out? I know it's out of respect for the dead and all that, but what's so respectful about taking your time?

So the car drives on and on. We sit in silence. We have a long way to go. Mum always said she wanted to be buried with her mother, and that cemetery is two hours away. I stare out the window. Mum and Dad were driving along this road when the accident happened. I wonder where it happened precisely. Do I want to know?

We finally get to the church. It's a cute little old

building made of big chunks of sandstone. I step out onto the grass and walk over to Tracy. She ignores me. It's hot and still and quiet. I think if she looks at me she'll cry and not be able to stop. There's no one standing outside. So we walk into the dark, packed church, Tracy first. I spot the shiny brown coffin at the end of the aisle. It's just sitting there near the altar like an overgrown coffee table with a flowery wedding cake on top.

There's a big, black hole in my chest, and it's growing with every breath I take. My mother's in that box. I can't believe it. It doesn't make sense. How can she have been walking two weeks ago and now be in a box with ugly flowers on top? I was okay until I saw the coffin, I really was. But this is too much. I now have to sit here in the front row and listen to the minister talk with my mother's coffin so close by.

Wouldn't it be funny if she started knocking on the lid?

"Let me out, let me out. I'm not really dead."

"Oh, whew, Mum, you woke up just in time. The minister was going to start rambling on about God's will and all that garbage. Jump on out and join the party. Everyone's here!"

She doesn't knock and the minister doesn't stop.

The minister talks and talks and keeps looking down at us. I must say it feels pretty special being in the front row. Is that sick of me? Oh well, God can't punish me now. He's already done it. He can't punish me for not listening to the minister either. The minister's a nice man. I know. I've met him before. He performed the ceremony at Ronald's and Peter's weddings. He's nice but boring.

Anyway, how can I listen? Mum is in that box.

She wanted to die first, before any of us. Well, she got her wish.

I've got to stop looking at the coffin. It kills me to look, but for some reason I keep turning my head to the right to see it. I'm going to throw up. The colored light shining through the stained-glass windows is making me queasy. And the tears, I can't stop the tears. I'm being quiet about it and I have my back to everyone, being in the front row and all, so I suppose they can't tell. I've just got to make sure my shoulders don't move up and down in that crying way. But if I don't stop crying soon, I think it's going to get worse and I'll start wailing like one of those Italian women in black sack dresses and stockings with black shawls draped over their heads. The ones who throw themselves over the graves and all that. It probably would be good to be Italian right now. At least they don't have to sit quietly and act like it's no big deal. At least they think it's normal to show, really show, what you feel.

The minister is almost done, and Tracy made it through without shedding a tear.

I wish she were Italian.

Now we have to leave the church. I have to turn around and face everyone sitting in the old wooden pews.

I have to walk past the coffin again and back up the aisle. I'm still crying like an idiot and I can't seem to stop. I'm going to puke. I just know it.

I'm up the aisle and I don't know how I got here. I'm walking without moving. Everyone's looking at me with sad, quiet smiles. We're poor motherless children. *"Don't forget about Dad!"* I want to say. *"He's still alive!"*

I want them all to hug me, but at the same time I want to tell them to fuck off. That would be nice. All dressed like a lady in pink but acting like a ruffian in black. I don't think Mum would like that.

She wouldn't know, though.

"Her spirit is hovering over us right now."

Bullshit! I don't care what the delusional minister says, that crap is just for people who can't cope with the truth. The truth is she's about to be shoved in the back of a big black car, tossed around like a sack of potatoes while she's driven to a cemetery, placed hovering over a hole, buried under a lot of dirt, and then left lying there all alone while we go off and eat tea cakes.

It must be so lonely in that box.

I wish I could save her.

My driver is sweating in the hot sun and holding the car door open for Frances and me.

"Thank you, sir," I say, swishing my pink hem as I get in. I'm Auntie Mame on my way to the theater.

So now we're off to the hole in the ground.

I don't think I can stand much more of this. I want to

hold my head up high the way grievers do in the movies, but this isn't really like the movies at all. They got it all wrong. This is unbearable. It's nothing like my daydream or premonition or whatever that thing was, where I was braver than Joan of Arc.

We drive and drive, slowly following the hearse. I suppose that's the number-one rule at funeral driver school: drive like an old granny. Take the corners real slow, and don't speak to the passengers. All the cars around us know who we are, the grieving relatives, and they drive slow too. It must be contagious.

We're almost there. The hearse has just turned into the tiny cemetery on the hill. The grass is dry and yellow and crunchy from the heat. Mum always wanted to be buried on a hill in the countryside. Very *Sound of Music*. Except the hills aren't alive, they're full of dead people. I sing quietly to myself, "When I'm feeling sad / I simply remember my favorite things and then I don't feel soooo bad." Somehow brown paper packages tied up with string won't cut it today.

The car has stopped and Frances gets out. From here in the car I can see the hole and the green Astroturf stuck down on the ground around it.

I don't think I can watch them put her in there. I'm shaking. I don't know what to do. I want to ask the driver, but he's staring straight ahead. Maybe he's lucky enough to never have been to the funeral of someone he's actually cared about.

I'm going to scream. I can't move. I can't get out of the

car. I can't. It's so wrong of me, Mum, and I'm sorry, but I can't stand there and watch it. I'm sorry.

Tracy's walking toward my car, so I press the window button down. I tell her I'm unable to get out and be decent enough to go to all of my mother's funeral and she walks away. She seems almost happy. I leave the window down. There are flies buzzing around but I don't care.

It's my mother's funeral and lots of people are here, but only one member of our family is up there saying goodbye. I can see Grandma and Grandpa, but they don't count. I wonder what Dad's doing right now. Can he feel it?

Here I sit. Wearing a pink dress in a car with beige interior. God, I hate beige. It does offset the pink nicely, though. I can only just hear what the minister is saying, unless a fly buzzes past and I miss it altogether. I can see everyone on the hill from the waist up, standing around the grave. I can't see Tracy.

Oh no, oh no! No no no no no! They're putting the coffin in the ground now. I can see the men using those white rope things to lower her down. I can't sit here and I can't move. I can't do anything. There's absolutely nothing I can do.

This is it. This is the end.

My mother is gone. She's in a box and she's not getting out.

She's dead dead dead dead dead. She's hasn't passed away. She's dead. Dead as a doornail, six feet under, pushing up the daisies.

She's gone and here they all come down the hill crying and talking softly. Don't come near me, I tell them with my look. And they don't. I sort of wanted them to, though.

So it's done and we drive away.

It's time for my uncles and their wives to go back to their daily lives, and it's time for us to get back to ours.

Whatever is left of them.

I thought the funeral was meant to help, but I just feel worse.

I can't do this living thing anymore. It's too much effort.

I can't sleep and I can't be awake. I want to disappear from the world so I don't have to deal with the day-to-day. I want to die. Then I won't have to bother with anything. I know Trent might miss me, but after a while he'll see that he's better off without someone like me, someone who's miserable all the time. Actually, misery's not even the half of it.

God, let me die. Maybe I'll be hit by a car too. I can't seem to kill myself. I don't have a gun and I don't have the guts to stab myself with a kitchen knife. Maybe I could OD on something. Why can't I just go to sleep and never wake up?

It's been a week since the funeral, and my fingernails look horrible. I can't stop munching on them. It's worse than ever. I shouldn't care about my stupid nails, but for some reason I do. Mum always said biting would ruin my nail beds.

Well, *I'm* in control now. They're my nails and I can do what I want with them. There's no one to stop me. No one whose permission I have to ask. So three weeks after the accident, I go to a nail salon. I've walked past it many times but have never gone in. It's all white, with mirrors. The women in there look happy and pampered.

I ask a manicurist with long orange nails to give me even longer dark purple ones. She's not the manicurist I wanted—I wanted the younger one with spiky hair, but she's home sick.

I sit down in a white chair and the woman starts to file what's left of my nails.

"You have lovely nails, but I must warn you, they have a tendency to grow upwards," she tells me in a sweet, soft voice.

"My mum used to say that would happen if I kept biting them." Then it comes out of me before I have a chance to stop it: "She died in a car accident just over two weeks ago."

The woman is quiet for a second before looking up.

"I'm so sorry," she says before looking back down at my nails for what seems like a very long time. At least she's stopped filing me down to nothing. I feel like an idiot. Why did I have to ruin this potentially nice experience by telling her? Most people gossip with their manicurist, they don't drop a bomb on her. Why do I always ruin everything? I decide to act extra happy so she doesn't think I'm some poor, pathetic, needy, crazy person.

"Gee, these are going to look fantastic," I tell her, smiling brightly. "Why do you have to file the top of my nails? What's that funny smell? Will my real nails grow underneath? Will I be able to take these off one day and just have nice long nails of my own? Should I have pointy nails or square ones? I love yours. How long have you had them?"

Now I wonder if she actually believes me or if she thinks I'm someone who goes around saying shocking stuff to get attention. I've never thought of that before. Maybe people will think I'm making it up. She seems to believe me, though, because she looks kind of sad and awkward. She tells me she has a daughter my age. She seems like she'd be a good mother.

I pay and choose dark Morticia purple nail polish.

She's so gentle and fast with her brushstrokes that it's all over too quickly.

"Can I stay here while they dry? Do you have one of those nail-dryer machines?" She does, so I stay.

She sets me up and then walks out the back with her colleague to eat lunch. It's just me, the buzz of the little nail fan, and white, lots of white. And then I notice my reflection in all the mirrors.

Me, looking like a stupid little girl trying to be all grown-up and sophisticated.

I do feel like a new person, though. I can't wait to get to school and show them off. Julie is going to just die. Oh, I shouldn't say things like that anymore. It might happen.

I'm going back to work because I don't want to lose my job. We need the money. And I need to get out of the house.

I feel like an idiot putting my Cookie Man uniform on. I used to love it, but all of a sudden it seems so silly, so trivial. A frilly white apron over a blue and white checked tunic with puffy sleeves. And to top it off, a lacy white hat, like an old-fashioned candy seller.

I take the twenty-minute bus ride to work and people stare at me in my uniform, the way they always do. I probably should just get changed when I get there, but that's an even bigger hassle.

When I get to the mall, I put on my "Selling cookies is fun!" smile and get started.

My nice boss says he's so sorry and I say I'm okay and then we open the metal rolling door at the front of the store. I love this store. It's warm and sweet smelling and it's attached to a bakery next door, which makes it even cozier. All the bakery staff take our cookies home, and we get to take as much bread as we can eat. That will come in handy now. No matter what, we'll have bread and cookies. A family could live on that if they had to. People have done worse.

"Would you like to try a sample?" Smile.

"Here's your change." Smile.

"Ooh yes, I love the peanut butter ones too." Smile.

It comes out of nowhere. I finish serving and walk behind the huge metal cookie-making machine, where on a usual day I would stand and eat uncooked dough. But this isn't usual. I start to cry. I can't seem to do anything these days without bursting into tears at some point. It's ridiculous. I need to get some control.

"Are you okay, luv?"

I turn and see the bakery lady with the dyed red hair styled high on her head. The nest of hair frames her tiny face, and with her long eyelashes and blue eye shadow she looks like a country singer.

I try to act calm, but it all comes pouring out. The accident, Dad in the hospital, the funeral, Tracy, Trent . . . everything. We lean on the metal beam between the two shops and talk until I'm smiling again. At the end of her shift she gives me extra ham-and-cheese bread to take home. My old favorite. I get as much as I want.

Dad's getting better, so it's time for him to move to another hospital closer to home.

"How's he going to get there?" I ask.

"In an ambulance," Tracy says, exasperated. What did I think, we were going to shove him in the back of the red VW with his legs sticking out the window?

The new hospital is only twenty minutes from home and five minutes from Grandma and Grandpa's. It's nothing like the one he just came from. I'd only give this hospital a one-star rating.

In the first hospital he had his own room, but here there are lots of other men coughing and spluttering. It's miserable.

His room is beige, beige, and beige, and the floor is cold beige linoleum, unlike the nice carpet at the other hospital. His bed at the other hospital was wood (well, fake wood, but still); here it's cold metal. I guess I shouldn't complain. In some countries you have to pay a lot of money to stay in the hospital. In Australia you get to stay for free. Maybe that's why the TV commercials say we're "the lucky country."

Dad looks so much better, and the doctors say he's improving rapidly. He's still crying and apologizing all the time, but maybe this change of scenery will help.

Evelyn visits. She's just walked into his hospital room in a pretty floral dress, all made up with eye shadow, rosy cheeks and lips. I've never seen her wear makeup before. She's awkward and giggly. She has a bit of lipstick on her teeth. Should I tell her? I'd want to be told. Do I really want to add embarrassment to her sorrows right now? Sometimes maybe it's better not to know.

Poor Evelyn must be having a really hard time over Mum. Mum was always there for her during her many unhappy times. I really feel for her, pretending to be all happy and putting on a brave face for Dad. She must be going through a lot. She's known Mum and Dad even longer than I have.

I can't even remember how many family holidays Mum made us spend in the far-out suburbs for Evelyn's sake. When her husband hit her. When he left her. When they got divorced. When she couldn't afford decent food. When her three boys were acting up and didn't have a father to bring them in line. We were all there.

I wish she'd stop giggling and joking with Dad, though. It's sad. I think it would be better if she just cried and let it out. It must be getting to Tracy, too.

"I'm going to get a drink. Do you want to come, Erin?" Tracy says firmly, like it's not really a question.

"Can you believe her?" Tracy whispers the moment we're outside Dad's room.

"What?"

"You don't see what's happening? What she's doing?" she asks.

"What do you mean?"

"The makeup? The flirting?"

"What?"

"Forget it." And she storms off to the hospital cafeteria with me in the rear.

November 24, 1983

It's exactly a month since the accident. Life goes on. Math goes on. I'm sitting here trying to make sense of the numbers I've written in my notebook when Mrs. C-J's head pops up in the small square window of the classroom door.

Is it for me? Wow, what an ego I've developed! Not everything is about me and my misery. But somehow, I just know she's here for me. She looks strange, like a scared little kid. Maybe she's scared of my math teacher too. Nah, Mrs. C-J's not afraid of anyone. She has God on her side.

She knocks softly and comes in. Then Mrs. C-J and my math teacher, Mrs. Pike, walk outside. After about a minute, Mrs. Pike comes back in, looking at the floor. Before she says anything, I get up. All pens in the room seem to stop moving. I look at Julie, who smiles a sad smile. I then slowly pack up my things in my dirty canvas hippie "I don't give a damn" backpack. I can't decide if I'm glad to be getting out of math or not.

Mrs. C-J and I walk out to the corridor.

"Erin, I want you to come downstairs with me," she says, closing the door behind us.

"It's Dad! It's Dad, isn't it? You've got to tell me. Tell me."

"Why don't we go downstairs?"

"What for?" I say, even though I'm pretty sure I know what for.

"Just come downstairs, will you?"

"No. Tell me now. I'm not moving until you tell me."

"Please, Erin."

"Tell me," I say firmly, threatening a scene. "It's Dad, isn't it?"

"Yes. I'm so sorry. He's . . . he's gone."

"What do you mean *gone*?" I want her to say it.

"Oh, Erin, I'm so sorry. . . . He died this morning."

Before I really let myself hear what she's said, I quickly grab Dad's blue and gray checked handkerchief from my pocket and stuff it into my mouth. I scream. I think I'm going to have an asthma attack.

We walk downstairs, hankie held in place until I get to the deputy principal's office. Deputy Principal Edwards is a big teddy bear. He's all soft and cuddly, with a bushy brown beard. His clothes never fit right—they're always baggy—and his tie is always slightly undone and crooked. He's no pushover, though. He just rules with a smile and an open fist full of marshmallows.

Chris is sitting on the black leather couch chatting to Mr. Edwards like it's any other day. That's what we do now. When something new goes wrong, it's something normal.

I don't know what I think anymore. I don't know what I feel, either. I haven't cried at all, and I felt like I would a minute ago. Part of me just feels nothing. My life is ruined anyway. What difference does another death make?

When Chris sees me, he gets up and hugs me and we leave. It's like he's taking me out on this glorious summer day for an ice cream cone. We get in the car and I feel kind of special again. These thoughts make absolutely no sense . . . unless I have a heart of stone.

"I thought he was getting better," I say.

"Apparently a clot of blood went through his heart. He died this morning," Chris says as tears start streaming down his tanned cheeks.

I just stare straight ahead. Now I'm to blame for two parents' deaths. Why did I have to think that terrible thought? God really must think I need to be taught a lesson.

"But he was in a *hospital*. Can't they stop things like that?"

"It happened too quick."

"Idiots."

I knew that hospital was only worth a one-star rating.

* * *

We get home. If you can still call it that.

I walk in and see Tracy. There's nothing to say, so I pick up Trent and go outside.

Dad's been dead for half a day and people are starting to visit. It's just like with Mum. . . . The phone ringing. Lots of hushed voices.

Two of the first visitors to arrive are for me. Mrs. Stockbridge has driven Julie here straight after school.

Trent and I are sitting on Dad's varnished pebble-covered verandah. The pebbles drive me crazy, because you can't sit for too long without getting indentations in your legs and bum. If it weren't for these pebbles, I could probably sit here forever and never have to go inside.

When Julie and Mrs. Stockbridge arrive, Trent wanders inside, but I stay put. I don't want anyone in there to see how thrilled I am that Mrs. Stockbridge, an adult, a teacher, would care. I feel special, and embarrassed that I feel special. I know that everyone inside will think I'm a pathetic girl looking for a mother figure.

They walk up and sit on either side of me on the top step. It's a sunny day, a beautiful day . . . if I thought days could be beautiful anymore.

"You know, I really feel fine. I'm okay," I tell them.

I'm sitting here feeling nothing much at all. I'm smiling and talking to people as they walk up the driveway to the verandah to see how I am before going inside to see Tracy, Trent, and Chris. It's dark and depressing in there. The whole house has lost its heart. Even though it's hot outside, the house is cold.

Ronald, Peter, Gai, and Frances come and stay again.
Flowers and cards start arriving again.
The phone starts ringing again.
People say they're so sorry again.
It's the same as before. Same details. Different parent.

Auntie Connie's casseroles keep coming, now arriving in dark blue ice cream containers. She doesn't have any casserole dishes left. We have them all. She hasn't said anything, but I wonder what she's been using at home. I must remember to get those dishes back to her. We seem to be quite forgetful these days, but it's not right when it's with someone who cares.

We put the casseroles in the freezer, being sure to not let Auntie Connie see the uneaten ones. It's funny. We have a big freezer full of ice cream containers again, like when Mum worked at the factory. It's not quite as sweet this time.

Dad's funeral.
I opt for dark blue this time.
We go to the same church in the same cars and then drive to the same cemetery, where they open up the same hole so my parents can be buried together.
It's the same sunny day. The grass still isn't green, but the Astroturf around the hole is.

I'm not crying as much, and this time I get out of the car. I'm an old hand at this.

The priest says his "ashes to ashes" speech as they lower Dad into the hole beside Mum. I want to peek over the edge so I can see Mum's coffin and say I *did* see my mother buried, but I can't bring myself to look.

If only I had some of that Italian blood in me.

Then we're off to the wake for tea and cake and chats about what a jolly good fellow Dad was. And so say all of us!

December 1983

They say God helps at a time like this. *They* say we're praying for you. You smile and tell them thank you, as though you really believe what *they* want to believe. *They* want to believe God can help you because *they* know *they* can't.

It's a big business, this grief thing.

They say God is a comfort to all those who mourn.

How can you be a comfort to those you've made suffer? What manipulation! It's like having your wounds dressed by the person who hurt you. It's like the kidnapped girl thanking her kidnapper for feeding her and not killing her.

No, sorry, you're a bit late, God.

He's useless. He's a fraud. No, he's nonexistent.

God is hard of hearing.

Either that or he's like a child who only hears what he wants to hear.

I love you, God.

Bless you, my child, for I am mighty.

I can't see you but I know you're there.

I am here, Erin.

Please, God, look after my mum and dad.

Pardon me?

Please, God, don't let anything happen to them. It's all I ask.

Can you repeat that?

Dear God, please keep my family safe.

I think we have a bad connection. . . .

Dear God, please watch over my parents!

BEEEEEEEP! You have been disconnected. If you want to make a call, please hang up and try again.

Chris is moving in with us. Well, actually, he's hardly left since the accident. I probably should mind, but I don't. I'd hate to imagine what it would be like without him here. Just Tracy and me on our own after Trent has gone to bed. Scary stuff. I don't like to be alone with her if I can help it, and I think she feels the same. We don't know how to act around each other. I try to talk to her about the accident, but she refuses to acknowledge that it's even happened.

I sure hope Chris doesn't change his mind about Tracy. About us.

It's time for Ronald, Peter, Gai, and Frances to go home. Again. They all live near the cemetery. It must be hard to drive along the same road, past the same fruit stand that Mum and Dad were walking to that night.

When we wave them off in their big red truck, it's like a final goodbye to Mum and Dad and the events of the past month.

A few moments later I hear a knock at the door. They must have forgotten something.

"I'll get it!" I yell.

But when I open the door it's not Ronald or Peter. It's two men: a fat one with a notepad and a sporty-looking one with a camera.

"We're so sorry to hear of your loss," the fat one says.

I love how people say that, like we've just misplaced our parents and we'll find them when we clean out our closets.

"Thanks." Now I should just slam the door in their faces—that's what Dad said to do to the Jehovahs—but I don't have the energy.

"We're from the *Daily Telegraph* newspaper," Fat Guy says while the other one stands smiling behind him.

"Yeah, what do you want?" Now I'm angry.

"We were wondering if we could have a few words with you about your parents."

How dare they? Are they kidding?

"We really care, you know. It's not just because we want

to sell newspapers. It's not because we get a kick out of this stuff and want a front-page story with our names on it!"

"Like what? What do you want me to say?"

"Can we maybe come in for a moment?" The photographer moves forward.

"No."

"Can you tell us how you're feeling about your parents' deaths?"

"No."

"Is there anyone else inside we could talk to?"

"No."

I'm starting to enjoy this. I, and I alone, have the power.

"Look, we don't want to intrude, but it would be wonderful if we could get some photos of your family. Help people relate to what's happened," Fat Guy says, all full of fake understanding.

Oh, how tragic! They want some family photos so the world can know what tragedy looks like. What difference does it make? Does it make it sadder or something?

"Oh, look at the poor little boy with the sweet face who doesn't have a mummy and daddy now because they died being thrown into the air and then crushed by a speeding tow truck! Oh, and look at that teenage girl, look at how she's smiling in this photo. I'll bet she's not smiling like that now. And that gorgeous eighteen-year-old girl with the pretty hair. I wonder how she looks now? Poor things."

"No, sorry, this is a bad time," I say as I finally muster up the guts to slam the door.

I wonder what would have happened if I had let them in. Would it have felt good to tell them all about it? Would I have enjoyed having it in the paper for everyone to see? Maybe it would have been a positive thing. Don't people want to be in the paper? Don't I want to be famous? Maybe not that way.

It's two weeks since Dad died.

It's early morning, and our driveway and grassy front yard are filling up with cars. Everybody's here to help us get rid of the past. It's for the best, they say. "They" being Mum and Dad's friends, Chris's parents, and Ronald and Peter, who have come back for the weekend to help out.

Tracy and I are still walking around the house in a complete daze most of the time. Trent is playing at Auntie Connie's. We don't want him to see what's going on.

So they're all here and I don't care what they do, as long as they stay out of Mum and Dad's bedroom.

It's like a garage sale.

"Erin, do you want this?" someone says.

I'm too tired to look up, so I just say, "No, take it. I don't care." So they take it.

Ronald is in the garage talking to Tracy. "The garage is so cluttered. Let me take your dad's boat off your hands," he says.

"Fine. Whatever," she says, and walks back in the house.

But Dad loved that boat! I'm thinking.

"Ronald, I feel funny about the boat going," I say.

"Look, you'll never use it, and it will just get in the way and rust up. I don't think your dad would like that," he says with his hand on my shoulder.

I suppose he knows best. He's also taking Dad's gold-panning machine and plans to try his luck. I hope he has better luck than Dad. I don't know what we'd do without him and Peter. He's probably going to quietly sell the boat to save us the hassle, and send us a check. I don't like the idea of selling Dad's boat, but I don't want it to die a rusty death either.

People have brought trucks and station wagons to clear stuff out. We don't even want to know about it.

"Take what you want," Tracy says. We're just too tired to care.

It takes the whole weekend with people coming and going. We're oblivious after a while. We're too busy trying to get through each hour. We're walking around like we don't know what's hit us.

It's nice to have people here. They're all so positive and helpful.

By the time everyone's gone, we're free from a lot of memories.

Some things are only gone temporarily. We've lent out some furniture to some friends of Mum and Dad's, thinking we might like the pieces back someday when we decide we want to remember.

"Don't worry. We'll look after it, and the minute you want it back, just let us know," they say.

Everyone drives off with their cars full, and then Dad's parents arrive. We go outside on the front lawn, hoping they won't want to come in.

"You girls have no idea of *our* suffering. You lost your parents, sure, but we lost our only child!" Grandma dramatically howls.

She then tells us they want Trent to live with them. Anyone would think Trent's a doll we've outgrown. I could understand if they were here for a piece of furniture . . . but Trent?

"You can't take care of him. He needs us," Grandpa says in his usual yell while his stupid white poodle barks from his car.

What, so you can beat him up the way you did Dad? I think. Mum once told me that they were the reason Dad found it hard trying not to get angry all the time.

"He's staying with us!" Tracy says.

"Not if we can help it. You don't know how to bring up a child!" Grandma snaps.

"Yeah, just try taking him away," I say, feeling tough and strong and ready to fight.

"He should be with us," Grandma says. "And he will be. The courts would choose us over you kids. We'll prove you're unfit!" Grandma says.

Tracy is crying, so Chris steps down from the verandah. He normally tries to stay out of family matters.

"I think you should go," Chris says. "Now's not the time to talk about this. Everyone's too emotional."

"We'll be back!" Grandpa yells before whistling at the dog and yelling at Grandma to get in the car.

They drive away.

"They can't take Trent, can they?" I'm in a panic.

Tracy turns to Chris. "Assholes! Shit! I'll have to go and sign legal custody papers first thing Monday. I should have done it already!"

Mum would die a second death if she knew Trent was going to be brought up by Grandma and Grandpa. They always hated Mum, thinking she wasn't good enough, and always tried to get Dad to leave her. Actually, I think they hate everyone but Trent . . . but give them time. Why did we have to get such horrible, weird grandparents?

I'll never forget the time Mum tried to put on a fancy lunch for them in an attempt to make family relations better.

Right before lunch, Grandpa went to the backyard, in the heat of the day, and with his bare hands picked up his dog's bubbling, blistering poop.

He then walked in without washing his hands and sat at the table for lunch. We all just sat there as he reached into the bread basket with his filthy, smelly hands.

"Looks like we're having Nutella with our bread today," I said, trying not to laugh.

I never understood why Dad, all six feet two and two hundred and fifty pounds of him, said nothing. Said nothing when Grandpa was rude to Mum, Tracy and me. Our dad, who could yell and scream at the slightest thing, just sat there in his own home while it was being smeared with shit.

Going to their house was even worse.

It was always a fight between Tracy and me as to who would have the misfortune of knocking on the door and being greeted first. As the younger (before Trent was born), I was usually stuck with it.

"Just give the old bugger a kiss and you'll get some pocket money," Mum would whisper with a smirk.

"Yuck. No way." Then he'd open the locked white metal screen door and I'd think of the roller skates I so desperately wanted.

"Yeah, come in, then!" Grandpa would yell before I'd plunge toward him, close my eyes, and hold my breath to kiss him on his dirty, stubbly cheek with food crumbs stuck to it.

"Here's a bit of something for you to spend," he'd say, handing me some coins from his dirty hands.

Mum and Dad would wink and Tracy would feign puking, having decided years before that for fifty cents it just wasn't worth it.

Then it was lunchtime. I'd get dry heaves throughout the meal imagining what I was ingesting off their dirty plates while watching Grandpa ingest boogers.

With Mum and Dad there I could eat the way I liked, with my fork in my right hand and my knife in my left. But when it was just me and the doting grandparents, it was "Ya right 'anded, so eat right 'anded," followed by a whack on the back of the head.

The worst part of the visit was going to the bathroom. Although they have lots of money, they use newspaper instead of toilet paper because of the Depression and the war. They were a long time ago, but Grandma still blames them for everything. The murky pink bathroom tiles definitely look like they're from the war.

"Back when we had nothing . . . in our day . . . we struggled, you know. . . . You don't know how lucky you are."

"But you have money now," I'd say.

"No, we don't. Who told you that?" Grandma would snap.

But they do. They own their house and have hundreds of thousands in the bank and lots of cash buried in socks around the house and in the backyard. Despite this, they don't flush the toilet every time, as "It's a waste of water and water costs money, you know."

There's also a metal potty next to the toilet that you can take into your room at night if you want. Lucky for me, I've only ever been there in daylight. There's no way I'd sleep on one of their dirty, smelly mattresses.

Now, is that the kind of household Trent should grow up in?

Trent's going to die before his time.

He's going to go outside and be hit by a car. He's going to be kidnapped while we're shopping at the mall. He'll be on a school trip, run away from the preoccupied teacher, and fall off a cliff. He'll be eating his lunch and fatally choke on it because we thoughtlessly bought crunchy instead of smooth peanut butter and a peanut got caught in his throat.

If we're not careful, we might just kill him, and if we don't, the world will. It's just waiting for him.

I wish he never had to leave our sight. I wish he really were a toy and we could take out his batteries and put him in his box when we've finished playing with him for the day.

I can't let him walk ahead of me and turn a corner before I get there, because in that split second he'll be gone. If I'm tired, he can't go for a swim at the beach—what if I blink too slowly and miss the wave that's going to take him away, or the shark lurking, waiting for a midmorning snack? Trent's not big enough to be a full meal just yet.

Oh God, why do I think such horrible things?

I wish he were dead so I didn't have to worry about his dying. Did I just think that?

Every night I like to go in and check that he's still breathing. He's asthmatic, like me. I've learned children's CPR just in case.

I think I'm going to be the first fourteen-year-old in history to die of a heart attack. I can't sleep.

Mum's been dead for more than six weeks and Dad's been dead for two weeks and I still can't get a decent night's sleep. Do teenagers get stomach ulcers? Is this what parents go through? Is this what Mum meant when she said she'd die if anything ever happened to us? No wonder she always looked so exhausted. This protective thing really takes it out of you. I wonder if parents are so stressed out about their children's safety that they sometimes wish they'd never had them. Maybe it's just not worth the trouble.

January 1984

I'm going back to school again. But this time it's with two dead parents, not one.

I'm going back to school even earlier than people expect me to. I'm not putting that short, ugly, traffic-light green school uniform on again. I've earned that right, haven't I?

I don't want my stupid, fat, tree-trunk legs showing. Tracy's always said that people with legs like mine should wear long pants and skirts, and I trust her judgment on these things.

I'm wearing dark green slouchy men's work pants I got at the thrift store. They're "tough and built to last," it says on the pocket.

I need a big, baggy, oversized shirt to go with them, but I don't have one. Tracy doesn't either—all her clothes are designed to fit tight, tight, tight—and I'm not about to start wearing Chris's clothes.

I suppose I could wear something of Dad's. Would that be gross? Would a psychiatrist say it's a sign of something more?

If I want to do that, I have to go into their bedroom. The thought of going in there makes me sick, but I have to. I want a shirt and I don't really know why.

I walk down the hall toward their closed, cream-colored door.

I turn the fake gold handle.

The room has a thick air in it. It's like there's a silent echo in here.

When I walk in, it's like in horror movies when a person stands at a door knowing they don't have a choice, they have to walk into the dark room.

"Don't go in there, don't go in there," the audience says. But you just know they will.

The sheer cream curtains are closed, and a dull light is coming through them. The bed with the gold bedspread is perfectly made. Like it would be anything else, Erin, you idiot. They're not going to suddenly reappear and have a snooze!

Mum's books are on their wooden bookshelf at the head of the bed. I've always wanted a headboard like it, with a light and bookshelves with frosted glass doors in the middle. Mum's books make me angry.

I'm OK—You're OK. Easy for you to say, Mum. *How to Look Younger and Live Longer.* Yeah, that worked. Were you actually reading these?

I walk toward their double closet, which runs along the whole of one wall. Mum's crystal face-cream jars and ring holders are already dusty and it's only been two months. It's strange. I can do anything I want in here. I can look at anything. Not many kids get to do that with their parents' room. The dead sure don't get much privacy. I must be sure before I die to get rid of anything that will incriminate me or make me look like an idiot.

I find a shirt in the first drawer I look at. It's one of Dad's favorites. A half white/half gray polo shirt with a thin red line across the front, crossing my chest, my heart . . . how truly deep and meaningful. Very symbolic. It's nice and big, Dad having been extra large and all. I think he stretched it with his beer gut. A man with a beer gut who didn't drink beer. Strange. Wow, this shirt actually looks good with my pants. I quite like it, not that I thought much of it when Dad wore it.

I'm ready for school. I feel cool. I feel fuck you. I feel like one of the tough girls from school who sit at the back of the bus snarling at all the sissies like me in the front. No one would want to mess with me now. I don't care what happens to me, so just try it, bitches.

Everyone at school is looking at me strangely all over again. Another Mrs. C-J school prayer, no doubt. Or are they just admiring my guts at not wearing the school uniform?

They all seem to be looking at me and feeling sorry for me and whispering, *"There's the girl whose parents died. What a poor, sad loser."*

I'm sitting in the playground on the cold metal benches.

"Think you're better than the rest of us?"

It's three tough girls from the grade above me. The heavily tanned "we're so cool we spend our weekends screwing surfer dudes at the beach" type. The type who pinned me and threatened to flush my head down the toilet when I first got to this school.

"What d'ya mean?" I always tend to speak like an uneducated moron when speaking to real-life uneducated morons. It's actually out of fear that they'll think I'm acting superior and punch me in the face.

"What's with ya fancy nails and clothes?"

"I—I just thought they'd look good," I say. So much for tough and built to last.

"Think you're pretty gorgeous, do ya? Better than the rest of us?" says gum-chewing toughie number one.

"Ya don't know how lucky ya are," says toughie number two with the big red greasy zit on her left cheek.

Lucky? I thought having dead parents would release me from their trivial bullshit. I thought girls like this would respect me more. Isn't it cool to be a tortured teen?

"Ya don't have to answer to no one now," number two continues.

Hmmm . . . it seems not everybody at school got into

the groove of the mass prayer session. Some people obviously don't think I needed it. I've hit the jackpot.

"Yeah," says moron number three. "Ya can do whatever ya want now, ya can come and go as ya please. I wish I didn't have parents that I had to ask permission for stuff. I wish I was in your shoes."

"Yeah? Well, step right in. I think they'll fit ya nicely. They'll be a bit tight and painful at first, and you'll probably get a few blisters, but you'll get used to it."

I *wish* I said something like that, but of course I didn't. I'm just standing here smiling like an idiot. *Smiling!* Why the hell am I smiling, and why can't I stop? Say something, for God's sake!

"I never thought of it like that. It's not that great, you know."

Oh, that'll get 'em, Erin. Have some balls! Why can't I yell at them and tell them what I really think? What have I got to lose now? Why don't I tell them that I want to ask my parents' permission, that I want them to care if I come home or not? That soon enough I'll realize that wearing my father's shirt is a pathetic way to hold on to him? That every day after school I have to take three deep breaths before walking inside the house? Why don't I gouge their eyes out with my fabulous new nails? Why don't I tell them that every minute of the day is agony, and no amount of nail polish and no number of parties is going to change that? Why don't I tell them that I live in fear, thinking my brother or sister will die at any moment?

Why don't I tell them that going to bed at night is terrifying? That I can't close my eyes without seeing Mum's and Dad's bodies slowly rotting? That every morning when I wake up I have a second or two of forgetting before it all comes crashing back like I've been hit by a car and I have to go through the shock and horror of it all over again—before I've even had breakfast! That for the first time in my miserable, chubby-faced life I have cheekbones and don't want to eat because the thought of food makes me sick? Or that I'm tired and don't have the energy for all this and can't imagine how I'm going to get on with life?

Why do I just smile and walk away?

These bitches who think they're so great. Oh yeah, girls, it's okay to hear you complain about your terrible parents who won't let you stay out as late as you want while I can do anything. I can't even sit through a whole class without wanting to scream and run around the classroom before charging through the window headfirst.

It must be fun to be that stupid.

I've lived a more interesting life than this. I just know it.

I'm in history class. It's one of my favorite classes because all my friends are in it. We always get in trouble in history because we can't stop talking and laughing. We're laughing and I feel guilty, like I must not have really loved my parents.

Our cute blond-bobbed teacher, Mrs. Pry, is teaching us about old Russia.

I lived in tsarist Russia. I can feel it.

Every time Mrs. Pry holds up a picture of Tsar Nicholas's palace, inhabited by his regal but greedy family, I see myself standing outside with the rest of the poor angry peasants dressed in beige (God forbid), shouting for better conditions because our lives suck. Hmmm . . . maybe that's why I have such a deep-seated hatred for beige.

All around me I see what *isn't* in the picture my teacher is showing us: the cobbled streets, the dome-topped buildings that look like colorful ice cream cones. I smell the other stinky peasants . . . or is that me? Maybe it is me . . . the current me. I have been wearing Dad's shirt to school and to bed every night and haven't washed it, or my hair, for a while. What's the point?

I love how when it comes to reincarnation everybody says they were once a princess or an emperor, never a low-down poverty-stricken nobody.

A couple of years ago I watched *Doctor Zhivago* with Mum and felt like I'd seen it before. I'm still not sure if it was a rerun or if I really felt a connection to Mother Russia. Maybe Mum's Edgar Cayce books are right. Maybe we do keep being reborn. Maybe Mum was on to something when she said you can come back as a cockroach if you're bad and all that.

I wonder where Mum and Dad are now? Could they be the kittens at the pet shop, the newborn babies I see being pushed in strollers at the mall where I work?

I suppose I'll never know.

Anyway, if they were reborn, Mum would come back as a thin, glamorous movie star, and Dad would be a chef with a restaurant full of regulars who all say "Hi, Ron" as they walk in.

Tracy has to quit her full-time job at the hair salon. She has to drive Trent to and from preschool/daycare, so will now only work a half day a week at the salon and do private haircuts in our kitchen.

Chris is helping support us, working at a car body shop. Maybe that's where he takes out a lot of his frustration . . . hammering away at cars instead of us. Chris never gets angry or impatient. He's so calm. I wonder why a twenty-two-year-old guy would want to put himself in the thick of all this. He really must love Tracy a lot.

I'm working at Cookie Man on Thursday nights and Saturdays and will work full-time during my school breaks. We also get a small family allowance from the government for Trent, so among the four of us we're making almost enough to survive, as long as we're careful.

No new clothes (it's not like we're going anywhere, plus I like wearing Dad's shirt). No fancy food, like ice cream and chocolate (I'm not so into food these days; neither is Trent, and Tracy never was). Lights off when you leave a room (we were supposed to do that when life was normal, but never did). No long showers and no baths (except for Trent, but he's so little he doesn't use much water. Sometimes I put my swimsuit on and bathe with him). And (the only one that bugs me, because I like to have my own) borrowed, not bought, textbooks and novels.

It all runs smoothly. As long as nothing goes wrong.

"The fridge has stopped working," Tracy says on Monday morning after having just done our food shopping the day before. "If this food spoils, we're screwed. We don't have any food money left for another couple of weeks!" She's crying.

It's funny, she can cry for a fridge but not for her parents. I guess the tears are all the same, really. I know she's devastated too, I just wish she'd share it with me.

Chris is quickly on the floor trying to fix the fridge, and Trent brings out a blue plastic toy hammer. It's amazing how he can make us smile at the worst of times. Chris fiddles and Trent knocks his hammer on the fridge door but nothing happens.

"I'm sorry, I've got to leave for work," Chris says, getting up. "I'll call you when I get there."

He kisses Tracy and Trent goodbye.

"We'll just have to call Ronald," Tracy says.

Ronald is the executor of the wills. The wills were written when Nanny was still alive, naming her as the person to take care of us if something happened. Now that she's gone, it's passed on to Ronald.

Tracy was furious when we found out. "I can't believe they didn't change their wills. I should be the one looking after this!"

So Ronald is in charge of the little bit of savings

Mum and Dad had after their debts were paid, as well as any money that might come from the possible court case against the driver who hit them. It's all blood money, if you ask me.

"Hi, Ronald. It's me, Tracy. . . . Good, thanks. Well, actually not really. Our fridge has broken down and it's full of food . . . . Could you please put some of our money into my account so we can get it fixed before everything defrosts? . . . Yes, Chris tried to fix it before leaving for work, but it's still broken. . . . Please, Ronald, all our food is going to be ruined. . . . What? What do you mean it's not the kind of thing the money is for? If you don't want to think of us, think of Trent, for God's sake! We don't want to lose him. . . . What if the courts find out we don't have food for him? Grandma and Grandpa will come and take him. Please, Ronald, we won't have any food left and we can't afford to buy more until next month. . . ." She's starting to cry. "So that's it then, you won't give us our own money? *Fine!*"

Tracy slams the phone down.

"Let me talk to him," I say, grabbing the phone.

"Don't bother, Erin. He won't do it. 'I'm doing this for your own good,' he said."

"So what does he expect us to do?" I ask.

"God only knows," she says.

Our suddenly stupid uncle seems to think that depriving us now will leave us with more for the future. But what the hell kind of future will we have if we don't get through the now part?

It doesn't make sense that he's being stingy with our money. Mum would be furious if she knew. She always said that if someone was tight with money, or obsessed with it, you couldn't trust them. They didn't have giving hearts.

"There's nothing worse than stinginess, in my book. . . . It says a lot about a person," Mum often said.

She's right; I'm beginning to notice that the ones with money are always the stingy ones, and the poor people are the ones helping others with the little they have. It's all upside down.

"Maybe we could call a repairman and tell him our situation and he might let us pay later," I suggest.

"No, that won't work. . . . Just let me think," Tracy says in a tone that tells me to be quiet for a minute.

So she thinks, and I go to the broken fridge and look around in the dark for Trent's breakfast. He's now in the living room watching cartoons.

"I don't want to do this," Tracy says, "but we're going to have to ask someone for a loan to get it fixed before we lose all the food. God, this is so wrong that we have to do this when we have the money, but bloody Ronald won't let us touch it."

"Who can we go to?" I ask.

Tracy looks miserable. "We'll have to ask Auntie Connie and Uncle Steele."

"I'll go up and ask," I say. How much more shame could we possibly feel?

"No, you don't have to do that. I'll go. It's my responsibility."

"No, it's not, it's *our* responsibility. It's fine. I'll go, I want to," I say, running into my room to get out of my pajamas and out of the house before she decides to go up herself.

I'm walking up the hill to Auntie Connie's place once again. I seem to do this walk a lot. She's sure to be sick of us by now, but we don't know what else to do. I ring the doorbell and she greets me with her usual big open smile and even bigger hug. It's weird coming to this house; it's so full of love, yet there still lingers some of the coldness from that horrible night.

"Hi, Erin, come in, come in."

I tell her about the fridge and Ronald, and before I even have to humiliate myself by asking, she's got her wallet out.

"We'll pay you back as soon as we can, as soon as we all get paid."

"There's no need for that," Auntie Connie says.

"Auntie Connie, I'm not taking it unless you promise you'll let us pay it back!"

Auntie Connie and Uncle Steele own a gas station and act to us like they have all the money in the world, but if that were the case, they'd have a swimming pool.

"There's no need to pay it back, but okay, if you insist."

"Thank you so much, Auntie Connie, I don't know what we'd do without you." Now I'm crying like an idiot.

"Don't be silly, we love you so much. It makes us feel good to be able to help. I wish we could do more."

I don't understand how a neighbor can be more caring than our own family and Mum and Dad's friends. We haven't heard from anyone in weeks.

Who said blood is thicker than water? They obviously had strange blood or didn't know much about water. As I learned in biology, we have a lot more water in our bodies than blood.

I walk back down the hill with two hundred dollars hidden in my hand. I hate the feel of it, but I must think of Trent's little tummy, if nothing else.

"Auntie Connie loaned it to us. She wanted to give it to us, of course!" I tell Tracy, who's sitting at the kitchen table with Trent on her lap and a stack of bills in front of her.

"I know. She just called. God, I hate this. I've called a repair place, they'll be here in an hour."

"Thank goodness. Well, I'd better get ready for school."

"Oh, Erin!" Tracy says, looking at the clock. "You'll be late."

"I don't care," I say with defiance. I'm late all the time now. They don't bother me about that kind of stuff anymore.

"Let me drive you when I take Trent to school," Tracy says really kindly.

"Nah, honestly, it's no big deal."

"Erin, please let me." She's almost crying again.

"Okay."

It's strange. Tracy and I get along best when something goes wrong—something outside of ourselves, that is.

I get dressed and Tracy gets Trent ready in his shorts and shirt. We all get in the red Beetle and it feels like family.

At Trent's school, our old school, we walk him to class, me on one side, Tracy on the other, holding his soft little hands. He looks up at us and smiles and we look at each other and do the same. We start swinging him in the air between us, and he giggles uncontrollably. I feel like I'm in a gushy movie, and I hope it never ends. Or at least that there'll be a sequel. We then drive to my school, which is about five minutes away.

"Tracy, this is the wrong gate."

"Damn it, Erin! Look at the traffic. Can't you just get out here!" she says impatiently.

Me and my big mouth! Why do I always have to spoil things?

I start to say "Good luck with the fridge," but she drives off before I get the whole sentence out. I don't want to go to school, but I guess I have to. I'm going to give us a future where if a fridge breaks, we can afford to fix it.

The next week when Julie is over to do homework with me, we decide to take precautionary measures after we go to the minifridge (which is only big enough for a few beer cans) behind Dad's bar and notice the freezer is iced up.

"Do you think we could fix it?" Julie says.

"I'll go to the garage and get a hammer or something,"

We start chipping away at the ice and I hit metal, and the fridge stops humming.

"Oh shit! Something's wrong. Tracy's going to kill me."

"I'll tell her," Julie kindly offers.

"Then she'll just kill you *and* me."

I go to Tracy, who is in the kitchen cutting a client's hair. She's making more money doing it at home than at the salon.

"Tracy . . . I'm so sorry, I was just trying to help."

"What? What did you do?"

I tell her and she just shrugs and says don't worry about it.

This can't be true. Maybe she isn't mad because it's Dad's fridge and she's more angry at him than at me. Or maybe she's trying too, and some days it's easier than others.

When the client goes home and Julie's in my room studying, I ask again, just in case.

"You're really not angry?"

"No, Erin, I'm not! I don't give a damn about Dad's stupid fridge."

Now seems like the perfect time to ask Tracy something I've been dying to ask.

"Tracy, I know you probably don't want to talk about

it, but . . . what did Dad say to you that time in the hospital before he died?"

Dad had asked me to take Trent for ice cream so he could speak to Tracy alone. At the time she said he just wanted to talk about practical things like money and Trent, but I had a feeling it was something more. Tracy appeared strangely sad after it.

"He cried and cried and said he was sorry for the way he treated me."

Dad was always horrible to Tracy and she hated him. When he would force us to do things, he would yell at me, but he'd yell louder at her. When it was homework time, I would work in my room, but Dad would force Tracy to sit with him at the dining room table while he berated her for not understanding. She would cry and he would yell and I would sit in my room and cry for her while guiltily feeling relieved it wasn't me.

"How do you feel about him now?" I ask.

"I don't know. But what about you? Don't you remember him kicking the shit out of you? You were about six or seven."

"No. What do you mean?"

"When you left your bike in the driveway and he ran over it. He stormed in the house and really laid into you. You were lying on the floor watching TV and he started kicking you in the stomach over and over again. It was awful."

"I sort of remember something like that."

"Yeah, well, Erin . . . that was our dad."

*　*　*

117

I get home from school and the house needs vacuuming. I promised Tracy before I left this morning that I'd do it when I got home, but I want to do my homework first. I can't fail at school on top of everything else.

I'm almost done writing an essay when I hear Tracy arrive home.

Oh no! I haven't vacuumed yet!

Tracy is in the kitchen clanking and clunking dishes. I run out.

"Did you vacuum?"

"Oh, Tracy. I haven't yet."

"Fine. I'll do it myself."

"I'm going to do it. I was just finishing my homework."

"Just forget it, Erin. I'll do it myself."

I run to the closet to get the vacuum and she snatches it from me.

"Erin, I asked you to do it and you didn't, so don't worry."

I tell her I'll do it now, but she won't let me.

"Erin, stop making it worse. Just go back in your room!"

"Please, Tracy. I'm sorry. I'm begging you. Please let me do it. I can do it right now." I start crying, and that makes her angrier.

"Stop blubbering. Now go away!"

So I sit in my room, with a sick feeling in my stomach, and listen to the sound of the vacuum cleaner. It sounds like what I imagine a hurricane might sound like.

*   *   *

We're all going to see a psychiatrist!

The lawyers want to get us while we're fresh. There's going to be a court case, and they need to know how affected we are.

Even Trent has to go. I hope they don't decide we're unfit to look after him.

I wonder if Tracy and I'll get to lie down on a brown leather couch and look at the ceiling. I don't want to go but am kind of excited at the same time. Secretly I hope the doctor discovers I have insurmountable problems, that I'm a complete loony and I need to keep seeing him. That I'm such a tragic case he'll definitely need me for follow-ups. I quite like the idea of talking to a stranger. Why do I think sick stuff like this? Here's me thinking I'm not really a loony, hoping he'll think I am, when maybe the truth is I am nuts and don't even realize it. Don't they say that crazy people don't know they're crazy? I'm doomed either way. I can't win. Either I am crazy, or I'm sick enough to want to be seen as crazy. Attention-seeking behavior, they call it. How humiliating to be so transparent.

I'm not so excited now we're here. It's just like a regular doctor's office . . . not dark and brooding and glamorous at all. I thought it would be all wood and leather sofas, but the waiting room walls are white and the metal chairs have gray vinyl cushioning.

Tracy goes in first while Trent and I sit in the dreary waiting room.

After twenty minutes it's my turn. As I go in, Tracy

says, "Don't hold back. Say everything," which is weird coming from her. She's always telling me to shut up about Mum and Dad.

I go into the psychiatrist's tiny, cluttered office. He doesn't even have a couch for me to lie on. I sit in a wooden chair. He's sitting behind his big brown desk that takes up most of the room. I feel like I'm going for a job interview, except that when you go for a job they look at you a lot to see if you're honest and all that. This guy isn't looking at me at all. You'd think he'd be looking for the madness in my eyes or to see if I have any twitches or anything. But no, all I can see is his profile, which isn't a pretty sight . . . a big red nose and a shiny bald head. The window behind him is closed and the brown curtains are drawn. It's dark and gloomy in here, and everything is casting a dark shadow.

"So tell me how you feel about your parents' dying," he begins.

I blab away and he writes in his big green book. I must get myself one of those. Then I could write my babble down and be my own psychiatrist. I'm speaking way too fast for him to be able to keep up, the way I always do when I'm nervous.

I try to slow down and breathe between sentences, but the words just keep sprinting out of me. I'm tempted to say something outrageous to catch him off guard, but I'd better not. This is important, the lawyers said. Because my parents weren't at a pedestrian crossing when they were hit, the tow truck driver isn't going to be charged with murder or manslaughter or anything, even though Dad said he was speeding. But Dad's dead now, so what does he know?

If Mum and Dad had been at a pedestrian crossing, the driver would be in big trouble and we'd gets lots of money, but they weren't, so he's not and we won't. I don't know why some people think money makes up for losing someone.

Anyway, the driver will be held accountable in *some* way, and we are to get some form of compensation. "Possibly," the lawyers tell us.

Maybe the more screwed-up we are, the better off financially we'll be in the future or something. Sick, huh? Or maybe they'll be tougher on the idiot who ran over Mum and Dad if the surviving relatives are fruit loops as a result of his stupidity.

I wonder what this asshole psychiatrist is going to make of me. He's so clinical and impersonal. He doesn't give a shit about any of this.

I never imagined it would be this way. In the movies psychiatrists really look at you, nod a lot, and say wise things. This guy says nothing, he doesn't give a grunt or a "hmmm." If I stop talking, there's a horrible, uncomfortable silence, and the only way to fill it is for me to keep rattling on (as Dad would say, I'm good at that).

It's a ploy; I'm not that stupid. I don't want to give in to it, but I can't stand how uncomfortable this all is.

I talk and talk; he writes. Maybe he's writing his shopping list. Maybe he's not writing my stuff down at all.

According to the clock I have ten minutes to go, and I don't know what else to talk about. For the first time since it all happened, my head is empty. I have nothing else to say about the great tragedy. Wow, this guy is good. He's dried me up; I have no tears left. As much as I want to think about the agony of it all, I can't. It's just not there. Where did it go?

I'm all better. It must be the great rapport we developed. He's cured me with his shitty demeanor. Is this some new treatment technique, to bore people with their own problems?

Thanks, doc, see ya.

Oh no, I've blown it. I probably didn't seem affected at all. He's sure to think I'm coping brilliantly, like no one he's ever seen before.

There goes the future.

I wish I could talk to someone who has been through it, someone who "gets it."

There's a girl in some of my classes at school whose mother died from cancer just after my mum died. I thought we could bond. I thought we could talk about our pain, but it doesn't work that way.

"Hi, Joanna. I'm so sorry to hear about your mum. If you need to talk to someone, I'm here."

We tried once, but we couldn't relate to each other.

Watching someone die a slow and painful death is different from losing someone suddenly. It seems how they died is just as important as the fact that they're gone. Maybe we have to deal with the *how* before we can even look at the fact of a life without our mums.

It's the school summer holidays, which means the end of my holiday from home, and all the memories, seven hours a day. Now there's no escaping.

I'll miss Mrs. Stockbridge, but she said I can call her if I need to. I feel funny and sort of a loser about intruding on her family and home life, so I don't think I will.

Lucky for me I have work every day. My boss said I could work full-time if I want to. I do. We need the money.

I've also got my theatrical career. I don't think it's right to go on the Shopfront England tour after everything that's happened, but Tracy says Mum would be disappointed if I didn't. So now I have a busy schedule, thank goodness. Work, then rehearsals, then bed, then play with Trent, then work, then rehearsals, then bed.

I'm now lying on the floor of the theater with a cork in my mouth. Errol, our director, says it's a theater exercise for diction and vocal projection. You put a cork in your mouth, lie on your back, and say certain words and phrases. I wonder if Elizabeth Taylor ever did this. If she did, she probably had that big diamond Richard Burton gave her in her mouth, not some dirty cork from an old wine bottle.

"You're going to be playing in bigger theaters than this, and you want people to hear you in the back row, don't you?" Errol says.

" 'Es, Ewal," we all say loudly through our corks.

Dad will think this is hilarious. He loves telling me to "put a cork in it" when I talk too much, which he says is all the time. Oops! Idiot. He's not at home. Why do I always do that? I have moments of thinking everything is normal. That Mum and Dad are just sitting at home like every other day. I really should just put a cork in my thoughts.

Auntie Connie is cooking a nice dinner for us, but I don't want to go. Tracy is angry with me for something. I'm not sure what it is, but the look of thunder says it all. So I tell her I'm staying home.

"God, Erin. Don't be so ungrateful," Tracy tells me. "She's doing this for us. Whether I want you there or not, you're coming and that's that."

We walk up the street. Tracy is carrying Trent and walking ahead of me in a huff. I feel like such a loser and I don't even know why.

When Auntie Connie answers the door, the bright light shines on Trent and a smiling Tracy.

"Come in, darlings," Auntie Connie says, and hugs each of us.

"Erin, tell everybody about the play." We're in the kitchen and now Tracy is being so sweet to me. The look of anger has been replaced with a gentle sisterly smile. Tracy turns to Auntie Connie. "We're so proud of her."

"Um . . . well . . ." I'm lost for words.

No. Hang on a minute. I'm furious! I want everyone to see how it really is between Tracy and me.

But they'd have to be behind the closed doors of 6 Knock Crescent, I guess.

Christmas is coming.

There is one joyous thing about this Christmas. The paperwork came through. Tracy is now officially Trent's guardian. Stick that where the sun don't shine, Grandma and Grandpa!

"What are we going to do about presents for Trent?" I ask Tracy and Chris before heading out to the theater for rehearsals.

"We'll have to ask Ronald. He can't possibly say no," Tracy says.

I know Tracy doesn't want to deal with Ronald after the fridge fiasco, so I offer to call when I get home.

"Hi, Ronald?"

I spend time making small talk so he doesn't think I'm just calling to ask for something. After a couple of minutes I ask.

"No! They'll cut my balls off if I give you money every time you want it!" he shouts.

Want it? We don't *want* it. We need it. He hasn't given us any of it yet, and I think Trent's happiness and continuing belief in Santa is a good enough reason. We have no idea who *they* are, but apparently they—the money police, I guess—will make him suffer if he helps us.

"Who will cut your balls off?"

"The lawyers who oversee everything I do."

"Come on, Ronald. Ultimately, you're in charge of our money. You can do what you want," I say.

"Presents are a waste! He's too little to notice, anyway."

How dare he assume that little kids don't notice things. What an ignoramus!

"I'm doing this for your own good," he says, starting to sound a lot like Ebenezer Scrooge. "I don't like to do this, but . . . no."

He hangs up and I call Peter.

"What's wrong with Ronald? He won't even give us any money for Trent for Christmas. Could you talk to him?"

"Erin, you're just going to have to trust him," Peter says. "He's doing what he thinks is right . . . what he thinks your mum and dad would want."

"They'd want us to have the money!" I try to calm down. "Look, Peter, I know he cares and thinks we'll appreciate this years down the track, but—"

"Okay, I'll call and see what he says."

He does, but nothing changes. Ronald's older, and what he says goes.

So we don't pay the phone bill. Fortunately or unfortunately, depending on how you look at it, the phone keeps ringing (they don't cut it off straightaway, giving you time to pay) and some other bills don't get paid, and Trent gets his goodies from Santa.

I miss Dad. He was always so fun at Christmas. When I was ten, the Lions Club Santa got sick, so Dad had to take over. I wasn't allowed to tell anyone, though.

The Christmas picnic was on the beach, so Dad—I mean, Santa—arrived on a boat ho-ho-hoing. It was exciting knowing my father was Santa Claus. Made me feel like the special-est kid around. I was the kid Santa loved the most, I was Santa's favorite. I wish Trent could have Dad be his Santa too.

Tracy and I took Trent to see the Santa at the mall the other day. We dressed him in his red, white, and blue short suit, and Tracy blow-dried his hair. His thick blond hair is now layered and wavy and flips back on the sides. He's a preschooler with a teenage hairstyle.

When we got to Santa, Trent walked straight up by himself. Not like all the stupid kids who were crying and carrying on.

"Hello, little boy," Santa said as Trent sat in his lap and hugged him.

"Hello, Santa." Trent smiled.

"And what would you like for Christmas?"

At that point Tracy and I froze. We thought he might ask Santa for Mum and Dad to come home, but thankfully he just said, "A big yellow truck."

Exactly what we'd bought him.

* * *

Thanks to those unpaid bills, we've got him enough stuff to fill a pillowcase. Just the way it used to be for us when we were little. Tracy and I would go to bed early, and I would be convinced that Santa's reindeer were above the house. Dad would leave Foster's beer for Santa and we'd leave cake for the reindeers before trying to get to sleep. Not for too long, though. We'd be up at five a.m. rummaging through our pillowcases, and then it was out to the cul-de-sac for all us kids to show each other what we got. We'd play until our mothers stood on our verandahs and called us in for breakfast. I wish it could be like that for Trent, but there are no little kids left in the street, apart from Auntie Connie's Peter.

We've put a Christmas tree up for Trent, but it's fake. It's made of plastic. Everything seems fake this year. We're really only having Christmas for Trent's sake.

Christmas used to be the best time of the year. Then something horrible happened and the holiday we loved the most became the worst time of the year. And there's no ignoring Christmas. Mostly because of Trent, and because people are singing Christmas songs everywhere. You can't go anywhere without hearing "Joy to the World."

Whose world might that be, I wonder.

It's seven o'clock Christmas morning, and I'm up with Trent looking at what Santa brought him. After about half an hour I tell him to sneak into Tracy and Chris's room so he can wake them and show them what he got. It's a great moment. It's like nothing bad has touched us. We're just a regular family on Christmas morning.

A few hours later Ronald, Peter, Gai, and Frances arrive. Even though I'm angry at Ronald, I'm glad they're all here. I'm tempted to talk to Ronald about the money stuff, but Christmas doesn't seem like the right time. So I show him Trent's presents, saying, "Look what Trent got. Santa's phone and electricity might be cut off, but *Santa* knew it was important that Trent still have Christmas."

We're all going to Chris's parents' place for lunch. They live five minutes away. I don't want to go, but I don't want to stay here either. Now that Trent's excitement has died down and we're quietly playing with his truck, the house feels sadder than ever without Mum and Dad, and it just gets worse when Grandma and Grandpa arrive to drop off presents for Trent.

"We can't think about Christmas without our Ronnie," Grandma blubbers while Grandpa scratches his flat bum.

Gee, he was never your "Ronnie" when he was alive. And since when have you given a damn about Christmas? All you've ever given us is blank Christmas cards so we can use them again the next year and save money.

They don't stay long, which I would say is our second

Christmas blessing of the day. The first being Trent's not yet asking where Mum and Dad are.

Chris's parents' house is messy and small. It's the kind of house that has a rusty, broken-down car parked on the front lawn and always has too much furniture crammed into it.

I don't know how Chris's dad gets around. He must bump into things a lot. He has MS and is in a wheelchair most of the time. It's strange seeing him get in and out of the chair. He wobbles like Trent did when he was learning to walk. It's sad and just adds to the sadness of today.

Chris's parents also have boarders from Korea and Vietnam. When Chris was living there, he had to sleep on the sofa so the boarders could have his room. His mum is a travel agent and likes the international feel of having Asian students staying there. His dad likes it too.

His younger sister, Katrina, is there. She goes to my school, but she acts like she doesn't know me. His older brother, Bill, and younger brother, Pip, are there too. Chris's mother is as plastic and fake as our Christmas tree. She's overly nice to people, then talks all nasty about them when they leave. I've even overheard her bitching about Tracy.

I'd rather she just say stuff to a person's face.

It's so hot in here. The oven is near the dining table, which is the type that extends to seat thirteen of us.

There's no dining room left. If you want to get out of your seat, you have to ask someone else to stand up, or crawl underneath, which isn't a pretty sight.

I miss being at Mum's dining table, even if it meant I had to be extra careful not to spill anything and drink like a lady with my pinkie up. I wonder what they'd do if I flicked some peas. Maybe Peter and I should teach Trent. Keep the family spirit alive. I wonder how Ronald and Peter are feeling having Christmas without their big sister?

Christmas is dead to me. I hate it. Pulling Christmas crackers and wearing stupid paper hats. Trent handing out all the presents under the tree . . . everyone acting so damn happy and everyone knowing we're just acting.

I hate spending Christmas in someone else's house.

It's someone else's Christmas. Not mine.

It's January 15, 1984. My fifteenth birthday.

It doesn't make any sense to have a birthday when the people who gave birth to me no longer exist.

It's dumb, idiotic.

I was born to Mum and Dad, and they're not here.

So I'm not having a fifteenth birthday. What's the point?

Maybe I am crazy. I'm definitely losing my mind. I'm starting to forget things.

I can't remember what Mum sounded like or how Dad

used to laugh. I can't stand looking at photos of them, so I can't even remember what they looked like.

Why didn't I think of this juicy stuff when I was with the psychiatrist? Why am I forgetting? What's going to happen?

It's starting to seem like they never even existed.

February 1984

It's a new school year.

Year ten. The year I can leave school if I want. Tracy hated school and left in year ten to be a hairdresser. But I'm going to finish through year twelve. I have to make something of my life to give this all meaning.

My new English teacher, Ms. Ockenden, is a staunch feminist. I love her class.

She introduces us to the great women of modern literature, like Virginia Woolf, who drowned herself by putting rocks in her pocket, and Sylvia Plath, who gassed herself by sticking her head in an oven.

It must be hard to be a great woman.

Ms. Ockenden has given us each a different book to

study and do a report on, as she says we're all individuals with varying tastes and talents. Julie was assigned *The Color Purple* by Alice Walker; I've got *The Bell Jar* by Sylvia Plath.

Ms. Ockenden hasn't said much about what's happened to me, but I get the feeling she understands me somehow.

She wants us to write about "childhood."

"You've got fifteen minutes. Don't stop and think. Just write," she says.

Everyone has their head down writing about the summer at the beach or about the day they got their first bike. I'm stuck. What am I going to write? Dead parents. Merry Christmas. Dead parents. Happy New Year. Dead parents. Dead parents. Dead parents.

I start to write and can't stop. I'm writing about death and coffins and skeletons and parents and more death. She's going to think I'm nuts.

"Time's up, pens down."

I don't want to hand mine in. I've exposed myself to be the idiot I am.

"Erin, what's wrong?" Megan asks. She's next to me on the wooden bench. I must look more depressed than usual.

"I feel so stupid."

We're all sitting outside at lunch. "We had to write

about childhood in English and I went on and on about Mum and Dad and death and stuff. It was full on."

Megan shakes her head. "That's not something to be upset about, Erin. It's good to express yourself in your writing."

I shrug. I'm not so sure.

Julie squeezes my hand. "She asked us to write about childhood. And you did."

We get our papers back the next day. I get an A+. Is that an A+, I pity you? Or an A+, you're brilliant! Somehow I think it's the former.

On my paper, Ms. Ockenden wrote, "Erin, maybe you should think about writing or journalism when you leave school." A nice compliment, I guess. I hope that after class she'll pull me aside to discuss my writing. But she doesn't. The bell rings and she looks down at her books.

Maybe it's like Megan and Julie said. Or maybe she's just embarrassed for me.

Maybe she'd just rather read about swing sets and happy families.

I swear I've watched too many melodramatic movies.

I'm having a diva moment.

It's ten p.m. Tracy and Chris are watching TV. Trent's in bed and I'm in my bedroom. I've just done something worthy of Bette Davis.

I got my aluminum tennis racquet and, John McEnroe

style, bashed my bed with its stupid orange chenille bedspread until I had no strength left. What a waste of time. It didn't do anything. The bed just bounced back. I couldn't hit hard enough.

I'm slumped on the floor with my hair hanging in my face. I don't know what to do to get this angry feeling out of me. Maybe I'm approaching it from the wrong angle. Maybe I should be hitting in, not out.

I stare at my beautiful long fingernails. Then I dig them into my skin.

Acrylic nails don't scratch.

The lady at the salon told me I could remove the nails by dipping my fingers in polish remover. I open a bottle of it and pour some in a cup. It works, sort of. My once-beautiful nails are dripping clumps of white goo. They don't come off completely. I have to rip the remains off using my short, stubby yellow nails underneath. I knew she was lying when she said they wouldn't harm my real nails.

After half an hour they're off. All traces of glamour are gone. Now I can get back to the dirty work. I have just enough nail to dig. Scratch. It works. A nice big red mark on my wrist. I like that my veins stick out more these days now that I'm not eating as much. That's a bereavement bonus right there. Scratch. I dig deeper this time. Yes! Blood. The pain feels good. Better than sadness.

Now my face. I scratch and dig my stupid childish tears and my ugly miserable face. I just want to scratch my whole face away so I don't have to look at it anymore. I won't exist as me anymore.

I look in the mirror. I look at what I've become. Oh my God. I'm an absolute mess. My face is all scratched up, all red and blotchy from crying. Welts cover my pale skin. I look like an albino mouse who's been in a fight with a cat and lost.

What have I done? Why am I really doing this? Am I doing this for attention? Everyone is going to see. I want people to think I can handle it. I don't know what I'm doing anymore. Why I do things. I never imagined I would be so desperate. I've got to stop. This is too obvious and pathetic. A Help Me sign around my neck.

It's morning and I'm sneaking out of the house with sunglasses on and my dirty hair over my face. I haven't washed it in weeks. There's no point when it will just get dirty again.

My friends tell me I should speak to someone.

"Erin, it's time to admit you can't do this on your own," Julie says.

But the teachers . . . can't they see that my face is all scratched up? Mrs. Stockbridge would, but she's sick today. Great timing, Erin.

I've been walking around school all day and not one teacher has said anything. Don't they think it's strange that I look like this? Maybe they're pretending not to notice. How embarrassing! It's obvious attention-seeking behavior, they're thinking. I must look like a fool.

They say a person does this stuff to feel physical pain, which takes your mind off the emotional pain. That's bullshit. You just end up feeling both. Great. Now I've got a throbbing face and I'm miserable.

Finally, toward the end of the day, Mrs. C-J, of all people, acknowledges the obvious. "Erin, what happened to your face?"

"Oh, I walked into some bushes on the way to school." I laugh. "Aren't I a klutz?"

I don't really want her to buy this. I want her to think I'm like those battered women who say they walked into a door.

"My goodness, have you put anything on it?" She touches my cheek, which makes me want to cry, for some stupid reason.

"No, it's okay. It doesn't hurt." Ask me more questions. But she doesn't.

"Well, be more careful in the future, Erin. You have such a pretty face." Yeah, right.

What? That's it? She must know I did this to myself. Maybe she's trying the "ignore the attention-seeking behavior" tactic so I'll give up. Maybe she does believe the bush story.

Maybe sometimes people have better things to think about than me me me.

I've finished my assignment for English class. I hope Ms. Ockenden doesn't think of me the way people did of Sylvia Plath. She supposedly wrote her book as fiction, but everybody knows it's about her.

I must say I'm rather proud of my work. I took a ring binder and covered the front with brown fabric. I padded the inside cover with quilted fabric and included all my notes on the misunderstood Sylvia. It's supposed to represent a padded cell. And the back cover is ripped and ruined, just as poor Sylvia was.

I can really relate to Sylvia Plath. She's incredibly unhappy and feels that no one understands her, and she's right. She doesn't wash her hair because she knows that it's silly, that you just have to do it again another day and another day. It wears her out like it wears me out. She sees that everything is so stupid when you only die in the end anyhow. She has trouble sleeping and then doesn't really see the point of getting out of bed in the morning when there's nothing to look forward to.

She thinks about killing herself and so do I.

"No matter how much you knelt and prayed, you still had to eat three meals a day and have a job and live in the world," she writes.

You better believe it, Sylvia!

Her father has died, but his death seems unreal to her. Plus, if he had lived, he would have been a cripple, just like mine. The similarities are amazing. There's even a character in the book named Mrs. Ockenden!

Was I destined to read Sylvia? Are some things already mapped out? I think so. I hope so. Maybe there is some meaning to things.

I love Sylvia and wish she were still alive, but I can

understand why she's not. Killing yourself can seem like the only way out sometimes.

I get an A+. This death thing really gets a girl good grades.

So the party's over. But where has everyone gone?

My parents' friends sobbed at the funerals, ate cakes at the wakes, looked at us with great sadness, and said, "If there's anything we can do, just let us know."

They seemed to mean it at the time, they really did.

Then they were gone.

I didn't notice at first. But after a few weeks I started to wonder why we hadn't seen anyone. The phone calls and visits just stopped. Of course, there's always Auntie Connie making sure our fridge is stocked with dinners, but that's it. I haven't seen Evelyn for ages, and she was Mum's best friend! She must be so upset and missing Mum that she just can't face us. Actually, everyone must be upset, because no one has come to our house since the big giveaway of all my parents' things.

I thought it would be like in the movies where all the adults flock around. You know, the community pulls together, making pies and stews, babysitting, coming over with cleaning supplies, saying, "Stay right there. I'll clean the house for you." The suffering ones cry from the joy of knowing there is so much loving and caring in the world.

People really come through at a time like this.

I thought Mum's friends would hug us and tell us

everything would be all right. I thought they'd offer advice and words of wisdom about being a young woman in the world without a mother. I thought they'd talk about Mum and Dad and we'd smile, thinking about Mum's silly mishaps and Dad's wheezy laugh.

"Remember the time they did this and that?" we'd say.

I mean, I know we're not the cheeriest house around and it must be a bit depressing for people, but aren't they even just a bit curious? I've spent my whole life around Mum and Dad's friends, and now they're gone. Well, not exactly gone . . . some of them live just around the corner.

They're gone to us, I suppose. I can't blame them. They've got their own lives. But . . .

I'm so glad Mum and Dad aren't around to witness the exodus of their lifelong friends. What a lie it all was.

March 1984

It's almost time for the Shopfront Theater tour.

I still feel weird about going. It seems frivolous and morally wrong, and just plain selfish.

My friends say I should go to honor my parents. One minute Tracy says I should go; the next, she seems angry that I'm considering it.

But Shopfront is where I had that horrible thought, and a week later it happened, though not exactly the way I imagined. Mum died instantly and Dad lasted a month. It happened, and I didn't feel powerful and brave and strong like I imagined I would.

Did God punish me for my thoughts, for being so evil

and self-serving? They say every kid imagines being an orphan. But how many kids actually become one?

I hate the word *orphan*. Everyone feels sorry for the poor little orphan. I'm not a pathetic orphan. My parents just happened to die, that's all.

Auntie Connie and Uncle Steele have turned their house into a circus-style casino for a big party in my honor. They've organized a surprise fund-raising event for the Shopfront tour. Qantas (the airline) is sponsoring us, but every little bit helps.

I can't believe how many people are here; I don't even know most of them. They're friends and family of Auntie Connie and Uncle Steele.

It's amazing. You can be feeling so unlucky, and the next day you're the luckiest person alive! The whole cast is here, and we're performing songs from the show. Trent is running around with his face painted like a tiger; people are playing cards, spinning the chocolate wheel, and having their future told for three dollars by Auntie Connie's cousin, who's dressed as a fortune-teller. I wonder what future I could get for three dollars. I'm too scared to find out.

I'm giddy with happiness. But I sober up quickly the next day.

"Isn't it wonderful, Erin?" Auntie Connie tells me. She's sitting at our kitchen table with an envelope in front of her. "We've raised five hundred dollars for you to go and have a fantastic time."

"Thank you so much," I tell her. "The kids will be so excited."

"What do you mean, the kids will be excited?" Auntie Connie asks, looking confused.

I tap the envelope. "For the extra money for the tour."

Auntie Connie shakes her head. "Erin, we all did this for *you*, so *you* would have some spending money while you're over there. Not the others."

I close my eyes. It was a benefit for me. But that's not what I'd told everyone.

When I tell Errol the next day at rehearsals, he's furious. "If we'd known that, why would we have come and performed?"

Maybe because people help each other out? But all I do is shrug.

"You don't need spending money." He is seething. "No one's taking spending money!"

"Well, I don't know what to do." This is so humiliating.

"Don't worry about it. It's your money. Do what you want," he says, walking off to the front office.

If it's fine, why are you acting so pissed off? I wish people would just say what's really on their mind instead of saying one thing but letting you know they're really angry. Assholes! I swear that when I'm older I'll never do that.

I don't want the damn money. It's not right. It's selfish to keep it all for myself. That's not the theatrical spirit.

144

"Auntie Connie, couldn't I just put half of it toward the tour?" I try one last time.

"Erin, it's not that much money to start with. Everybody who came that night came for *you*, not some kids they don't know. Kids with parents who I'm sure are giving them a bit of money to take along, I might add." Now Auntie Connie's getting annoyed.

God. Now everybody is annoyed with me!

I wish we'd never had the stupid fund-raiser.

We're putting on the show for family and friends before we leave for England. At least if we make a mistake, it will be in front of people who know us. In a way, that feels worse. I'd rather screw up in front of strangers.

I'm so nervous. All my friends are coming.

The lights have gone down and I'm onstage. It's strange. I have that feeling I had that terrible day when I thought the bad thought. I do feel brave and strong . . . sort of.

The lights are up and we're all singing. Our hard work is paying off. The show zips along, and then I'm in the spotlight, wearing tap shoes and mock-sadly singing, *"If I only had a dancing partner."* Everyone is laughing, thank goodness. I wasn't sure if I had it in me to be funny anymore.

Toward the end of the show I walk out deadpan, stare at the audience, and say, "Nobody loves me. Nobody even likes me. I must be horrible." I'm starting to understand why Errol gave me these lines. I've become that girl.

I can see my friends in the back row. They're holding a white banner that says BREAK A LEG! ERIN VINCENT SUPER-STAR! I am so lucky to have such good friends. I could never get through this without them. I know everyone says it, but I really do have the best friends in the world. They clap and cheer louder than anyone in the audience, and when we run offstage after the last song, they start stomping their feet, whistling, and chanting my name.

Mum would be so proud.

"Erin, that was amazing," Megan says when I go out to greet them.

"Speech! Speech!" Meredith shouts.

Julie begins imitating a Hollywood movie star. "I'd like to thank God, my fans, my parents—" She claps a hand over her mouth, horrified. And my tears come.

Why do I have to cry now?

"Oh, Erin. I didn't mean to—"

"I just wish they were here, that's all," I say. Then I start laughing. I can do that on cue now that I'm an actress. We group hug. "Hey, but how many people get a rowdy crowd like you guys to cheer them on!"

April 1984

"Would you please hurry up? I'll miss the plane!" I'm shrieking.

My flight leaves in two hours, and everyone's here to see me off. Tracy and Chris and Trent, and even Ronald, Peter, Gai, and Frances.

"Calm down, Erin. They'll wait for you, for God's sake," Tracy calls from the bathroom.

"No, they won't! They're not going to hold an international flight just for me," I say, picking up my suitcase and putting it down again. Sometimes I think Tracy believes the world will stop for us just because we have dead parents.

Tracy is putting on makeup, Trent's not dressed, and Ronald and Peter are doing I don't know what.

I know Tracy probably feels bad that I get to go overseas while she stays here in the misery. I still feel guilty for going, but she keeps telling me to go for Mum and Dad's sake. "Look, you're lucky to get away from all this. I would if I could. So go!" she says.

I go out to the car and start honking the horn. Finally, they come. I'm in Ronald's red truck and Tracy, Chris, and Trent are in the VW.

"Could you please drive faster, Ronald? I was supposed to be there three hours before the flight and it leaves in an hour!" Mum and Dad would have got me there on time. I should say that.

Finally we arrive at Sydney airport. Peter grabs my bag and we run to the check-in counter.

"Erin Vincent. Erin Vincent. Please report to gate thirty," a voice says over the loudspeaker as the man at the desk hands me back my passport. How embarrassing! There's no time for goodbyes, which is good. I'm glad I don't have time to hug Trent for too long, otherwise I'd never leave. I'm glad to be getting away from all this, and at the same time I feel like I'm doing the wrong thing. It's not fair to Tracy. I'll bet she'd like to be escaping to England right now.

I hurry through security and run to the gate. I'm the last one to board. The flight attendants are beginning their safety demonstration.

Passengers stare at me as I look for my seat. It's the only one that's empty. I slink down the aisle to claim it.

"We were already reworking the show," Errol snaps. My eight castmates avoid my apologetic eyes.

I can't even look at Errol. Maybe they all hoped I wouldn't make it. A girl with dead parents sure puts a damper on things.

But I made it. I'll show them it was worth not writing me out.

I'm in London and it's cold and sunny. I love it here. I love being away from home. We're staying in hotels and also with families with children in the theater who have offered to put us up.

I have all this energy in my body. I suppose it's the excitement of it all. Errol doesn't like it. Ever since the casino night fiasco, he's been really cold toward me. "Stop being so manic!" he tells me. Since when has being happy and thrilled and energetic been a crime? I just want to show everyone that I'm fine. I'm not going to ruin the tour.

The problem is, I do sort of know what Errol means, but I can't help myself. I'm full of hilarity, laughing like a maniac a lot of the time. And my voice seems much louder than before. But for the first time in six months, I don't feel depressed and mopey.

I'm going to see so many things and meet so many people. I can't wait to go to Shakespeare's house and see some plays in London's West End and meet some actors and visit all the sights. If I can feel this good now, then I know it's possible to feel happy again.

We're on our way to Liverpool. I'll bet this Liverpool will be better than the Australian one. It's two weeks into the tour. I'm sitting here quietly on the bus in my jeans and sweatshirt, listening to my Police tape on my Walkman. My hair is in a ponytail and it's clean! I'm wearing lip gloss. I'm trying not to act overly excited or talk too much. From the outside, I look completely normal.

But I don't feel good. I need to talk to someone.

I lean across the aisle. "Liz, what are you reading?"

Liz is eighteen. She's the oldest girl on the tour. She looks up from her book. "The Bible."

"Oh," I say, trying not to sound shocked. Liz is really cool. What's she doing reading the Bible?

Errol asks the driver to stop the bus, and we get out and look at a bunch of rocks and stones. They seem to have a lot of them in England. So far we've seen Stonehenge, where the rocks are standing around in a pattern like someone very strong placed them there. Then we see Hadrian's Wall and lots of castles and remains of castles and more rocks. I should be thrilled to see all this history, but for some reason I'm not.

I'm having a good time shopping, though. Is that shallow of me? Shouldn't I care about deeper things than that? I feel guilty about the spending money, but Auntie Connie was right, the other kids have money.

I've bought some new clothes and tapes that keep my mind occupied as we travel.

Today Francine, the youngest girl on the tour, is the first to be dropped off with her host family. This is the first time we're to stay with English families. I'm really nervous. What will it be like to stay in a stranger's house?

We're parked outside a mansion that is like a mini version of one of the castles we've just seen. The family of the manor is standing out front to greet Francine. The mother, in tweed, has long blond hair, as do her pretty teenage daughters. The father is smoking a pipe—how very English!

We say goodbye to lucky Francine, and next it's Liz and another mansion. Then six more stops. Not all the houses are mansions, but they're all nice.

The bus pulls up in front of a cluster of row houses. Errol tilts his head toward one with a red front door. "Okay, Erin. Here we are."

"Ha, ha, Errol. Very funny."

Errol doesn't laugh. "I'm serious, Erin. This is it."

"What?" I can't help thinking this is part of his vendetta against me.

He taps his fingers on the armrest. "We'll be back in the morning to pick you up for the lunchtime show."

"Do they know about what's happened?" I blurt out.

"Yes, I thought it better that they do," Errol says as I take my bag and open the door.

For once, I'm glad someone knows. I don't want to have to explain it.

I'm standing on the wet street with my now-wet suitcase and shoes. The sky is gray, the grass is gray, and all the houses in this street, which are joined together and sit in a long row, are gray and cold. I'm having the dirt-poor English experience.

I ring the doorbell but it doesn't work. So I knock. A dark-haired lady wearing a flour-covered apron answers the door.

"Come in, luvvy, it's bloody cold out there," says the lady, who introduces herself as Janice and her husband as Ted. "My Danny isn't home from school yet. You'll be sharing his room. You don't mind sharing with a twelve-year-old boy, do you?"

I do, but I remind myself that I'm a bohemian artist. "No! Of course not."

It's now eight o'clock. I'm sitting on the family sofa squashed between Janice and Ted. Danny is now home and is sitting on the floor in front of us. It's kind of nice, actually. We've just eaten a dinner of fried eggs and chips with tomato sauce and are watching an English TV show, *Love Thy Neighbor*.

I'm waiting for the questions about my exciting adventure or the accident, but they don't come. Aren't they fascinated by the fact that they have an international traveler in their midst?

Apparently not. The show ends, and Danny and I are told to go to bed.

"I'll be up in a tick," Janice tells us as we climb the olive green carpeted stairs.

"Mum, I'm old enough by now," Danny yells, and then turns to me, rolling his eyes. "She likes to come up and say goodnight even though we've already done that."

I grab my pajamas and get dressed in the freezing cold bathroom and run and jump into my bed hoping Danny won't see me.

"Everyone set?" Janice says from the bedroom doorway. She tucks Danny in and he tells her to stop fussing before she does the same to me.

"You're a lovely lass, you know that? It's a real pleasure having another girl in the house. I wish you could stay longer than a couple of days." She smiles. "Now, if you need anything, just call. We're right in the next bedroom."

"Thank you, Janice," I say, feeling myself get all teary for some stupid reason.

I'll bet Francine isn't getting this cozy treatment at that big, cold mansion.

For a few days, it almost feels like I have a family again. When it's time to say goodbye, we all hug, and I promise Janice I'll write. There really are some good people in the world.

In Scotland, we're staying in a hotel. Liz and I are sharing a room. Despite the God thing, she's both hip and nice, and I'd really like her to like me. Not just as a grieving girl, but as me, Erin.

Our room has dusty pink walls and shiny gold bed-spreads. Very movie star! It's fun. Liz and I lie in bed and talk like we're having a sleepover, only we're in a hotel in Scotland and everyone back home is awake and walking around while we're going off to sleep.

"Goodnight, Liz."

"Goodnight, Erin."

Lights out.

I'm lying here. I can't sleep. For some reason I feel shaky. Scared.

My parents are dead.

I feel like I want to jump out the window. My head's about to explode. I'm in a big fat panic and I don't know what to do. My body feels so weird. All these thoughts are rushing through my head. How am I going to live my life? How am I going to get through it?

When I was little, I'd often get a really high temperature and get delirious and Dad would put me under a cold shower, then sit with me and calm me down. No one is here to calm me down now.

I want to wake Liz. She's going to think I'm a stupid, crazy, mixed-up girl who can't even cope with death. People cope with death every day all over the world, so why can't I? I thought I was getting used to it.

But it's come back again, worse than ever. If I don't wake Liz, I'm afraid I'll go over the edge and I'll never come back.

"Liz," I whisper. "Liz." I shake her gently. "I'm so sorry to wake you."

She sits up like she was never asleep.

"I'm so sorry," I say as I pace around the room.

She turns on the lamp beside the bed. "Erin, it's fine. What's wrong?"

"I feel like the room's spinning or something, I can't quite explain it. I feel all shaky. Do I have a temperature?" I put my head down for her to feel.

"No, you feel okay."

"I feel like I just want to run around the room and scream. Is that crazy?"

"Of course it isn't."

She's just being nice. I know it's crazy.

She motions for me to sit down. I sit down because I don't know what else to do.

"Is it your parents?" she asks gently.

"I don't know." All of a sudden I start sobbing and I can't control it. I hate people seeing me like this. "Please don't tell anyone about this, Liz," I say through my tears.

"I won't. I promise."

"I just feel so depressed and frightened. Like I'm in a bad dream and I can't wake up. It's like I'm in shock over and over and over again. Like I just wake up and think, Oh my God, my parents are dead! Like I've just realized it for the first time.

"I just can't believe it, Liz, I can't believe they're dead. I can't believe that one minute they were walking around and now their bodies are turning to skeletons. It makes me feel sick. And why am I so jittery that Errol has to tell me to calm down all the time? I'm tired and terrified at the thought of tomorrow and the next day and the next. How am I going to get through this? I don't know what to do because it's not getting any better. I think it's actually getting worse."

So much for not talking and annoying people.

Now I'm really sobbing and blubbering, but I can't help it. I don't know how to describe my pain to anyone, because it doesn't fit any description. No words can say what I feel.

Liz just sits there and listens to me like I'm normal, like she's not shocked or horrified or embarrassed for me or anything. I talk and talk and talk. It's so nice of her. She's just on her bed next to mine in the middle of the night, listening. She doesn't act freaked out at all.

Finally I'm exhausted enough to maybe fall asleep.

The next morning she doesn't say anything about what happened. But I get the feeling that it's not because she doesn't care, but because she's leaving it for me to bring it up if I want to.

I don't want to. Because when I'm here in Scotland, I want to forget everything about October 23, 1983.

The tour is a big success. And then I'm back home. Tracy and Trent are at the airport to pick me up. Tracy's in a bad mood. I try to ignore it as Trent hugs me and asks lots of questions about where I've been, did I fly in the sky, that sort of thing. We get in the car, and if it wasn't for Trent, we'd be driving home in silence. Even at the age of three he's easier to talk to than Tracy. I guess I shouldn't be surprised. It's not like we talked or did much together before the accident.

Everything looks the same at home. All the feelings I've been avoiding for six weeks come flooding back. I try to tune them out. Things are going to be different now that I'm more worldly. I now know that there's so much more out there than what's in this house.

I'm home for less than an hour and Tracy's mad, angry, annoyed, and upset. I don't exactly know what about. All I know is it's worse than usual. I know why she acts like she hates me—because I got to go away. Because I'm back. Because she feels stuck with everything . . . me included.

I ask Chris, "Did anything bad happen while I was away?"

What a stupid question. Bad is a daily occurrence around here.

"No, nothing. Everything's the same," he says.

"So why is Tracy in such a bad mood? Is it me?"

"No, Erin, she's fine. She's got a lot to deal with, you know. Just ignore her."

But I can't. So much for absence making the heart grow fonder.

I wrote lots of postcards and letters and made phone calls, so she can't be angry at me for abandoning her. Can she?

I'm constantly on edge. Walking on eggshells. I had to walk on eggshells a lot with Dad, and now I have to with Tracy. She acts like a really angry parent.

I walk into the kitchen and Tracy turns her back to

me and starts rummaging loudly through the cupboards, opening and closing drawers really hard.

The mug says *I'm pissed!* as she slams it away. The bowl says *I hate my life!* as she reaches into the cupboard. The wok says *I hate you!* as she slams it on the counter.

Maybe I should write a guidebook:

GUIDE TO TRACYSPEAK
BANG: I hate my life and I hate you.
BASH: Why me?
BOING: You little bitch.
CLANG: Why did I have to be the oldest?
CLANK: I hate the sight of you.
CLUNK: Why haven't you cleaned this up yet?
CRASH: You got off easy.
SMASH: I want to kill you.

Before I came into the kitchen she wasn't doing any of that, so I know it's me she's angry at.

"What's wrong?" I ask.

"Nothing."

"Have I done something?"

"No," she says.

"Then what's wrong?"

"Nothing!" she says in that really short, stern way of hers of saying nothing's wrong but everything's wrong.

"Well, it doesn't seem like nothing. You seem really angry with me."

"I told you, nothing's wrong!" she says, getting more and more furious.

And then she storms off. I've been back three hours.

We've been through this before and it always ends the same. I'll be on eggshells for a few days. She'll be angry at me for a couple more days before eventually telling me that I left the dirty dishes in the sink or I did or said something I shouldn't have.

She acts like she hates me, which makes me hate her.

All I want is for us to be close. Why is she so mad at me? Why does she look at me that way?

Maybe I just have to try harder. One of us has to make the first move. I have to help Tracy. I have to be there for her more, and then maybe this won't happen. She has so much on her plate. I have to remember that. She doesn't mean to be like this. Maybe being angry is easier than being sad.

Julie is becoming an expert in Tracyspeak too. Like me, she can understand it but can't speak it herself.

"Why does she think she's cornered the market on pain? They were your parents too," she says in my bedroom after witnessing a kitchen conversation in Tracyspeak.

Even though I agree with her, I play devil's advocate. "I know. But I suppose she's got more responsibility than I have."

"It's not your fault they died and she was born first. This is awful. The door's closed, but I can feel the tension coming through the walls."

Julie seems to be getting upset on my behalf lately for some reason. It's kind of nice.

"Maybe we should go to your place," I say.

Julie's not crazy about her house. It's small, and she has to share her room with her little sister. But it's better than my house. So we pack up my schoolwork and some clothes and ask Chris (I don't dare ask Tracy) if he can drive me to Julie's so I can stay at her place for the night.

"Sure," he says in his usual calm manner. Maybe he's relieved. Maybe I should have stayed in England for good.

It's Monday and back to school again, but this time I'm doing it in style—London style, that is. At least for today.

I've got on my huge industrial-sculpture silver earrings, green neon socks and black high-heeled boots, neon orange fishnet gloves, black pants, and my favorite tour purchase—a white floor-length coat with pink, orange, green, and black splashes all over it. And to top it all off, I've got my London haircut, short on one side, long on the other.

Trent comes into my room as I pack my school bag. "You look pretty, Erin."

"And you look very handsome," I tell him as he stands there in his pale blue pj's.

I can't wait for Tracy to see me.

"You're wearing that?" she says as I walk into the living room.

"Yeah, why?"

Tracy snorts. "Well, have you looked in the mirror?" She shakes her head. "Can't you just be normal for once!"

Now I feel stupid. Then I remember that Tracy hasn't been to London and seen all the fashion, so she doesn't get it . . . yet.

Everyone at school is looking at me, but this time it's for a good reason. You can't buy clothes like these in Australia, so I'm ahead of everyone else.

"Hey, Erin, where do you get those cool socks?" "That's the best coat ever, I wish I had one!" "Oh, Erin, you look absolutely bloody fantastic!"

I go to class dressed like this because I can. I might look great, but I still have dead parents. The teachers are probably thinking, *Well, at least she looks clean and isn't wearing her father's shirt.*

Ms. Ockenden says that in a week each of us has to give a presentation about a character from Chaucer's *The Canterbury Tales.*

"Be creative!" she says.

I choose the Wife of Bath. Seems fitting, considering I've just been to Bath in England, and for a while there before the tour I was in a serious need of a bath.

I love the Wife of Bath. She doesn't care what anyone else thinks of her or the way she looks. She's dirty and bawdy and she knows what's what.

I decide to try to become the Wife of Bath. My acting chops are still warm from the trip, so I'm primed. I have one week to learn lines and create the costume of an ugly, grotesque, haggard old lady. Gee, and I was only just starting to dress better.

It's the day of the presentation and I'm in the hall. I'm the last to go, as I take the longest to get organized. No one else has done the costume thing like I thought they would. Most people get up and read from their papers like they're standing behind a podium. I'm starting to worry about my choice, but it's too late now. I've got a big padded butt (two towels pushed down some pantyhose) saggy boobs (my bra is stuffed with tea towels), dirty rags (bought at the thrift store and rubbed in the dirt), blackened teeth, and hair cut from my head and stuck on my chin.

I burst through the door as the Wife of Bath in all her burping, crotch-scratching, farting glory. Sorry, Mum, this is no time to be lady.

"You all think ya know me, but ya don't." *Burp!* "I might not be the prettiest lass in town, but I'm the smartest." I tell them all off for thinking I'm a dirty old hag and not looking any closer.

At the end of it I'm quite pleased with myself, but I can tell some of the girls think I'm a weirdo.

I feel like screaming at them.

It's official. I'm an idiot and I can't help myself. I want to be smart and creative and express myself. Okay, so maybe dressing up like a dirty old hag was a dumb idea, but at least I tried. Julie gets it. She loves it. So does Ms. Ockenden.

"That's what I mean when I say I want you all to present something and express yourself," she says, clapping. Now I feel like a dorky teacher's pet. She's probably only carrying on this way to encourage the parentless girl. I'll bet the teachers have been told it's good if I get involved in class activities.

"Everyone thinks I'm an idiot," I whisper to Julie when I'm done.

"No way! That was bloody great. Stick it up their arses," Julie says in true Wife of Bath style.

I do feel pretty stupid, though. For all my ranting and raving, they're right. I feel like a show-off and a loser. Not an artist at all.

Ultimately, Chaucer really pisses me off.

I have a toothache. Maybe I got too into the whole Wife of Bath bad teeth thing. Am I one of those Method actors who really feel everything they act? Or maybe it's all those English chocolates I ate on the tour.

Whatever it is, it hurts. We can't afford things like expensive dentist visits. Maybe it will go away if I ignore it.

It's a day later and my mouth is starting to swell up. I'm starting to talk like Marlon Brando in *The Godfather*.

I call Ronald and tell him. I hope he can hear how strange I sound.

"Have you been looking after your teeth?" he asks me.

"Yeah, of course."

"Well, then it will probably go away in a few days. I

can't just give you money every time you call and ask for some."

"But I hardly ever call," I protest. "If it gets worse, it could cost a lot more!"

"Erin. Just relax. I'll bet it will go away."

"Thanks a lot, Ronald!" I say with spit dribbling from my sore mouth as he blabs on about doing this for my future.

"I can't wait. I'll be a rich, toothless lady one day and it will all seem worth it," I say, fighting back tears. Mum would be so pissed with him!

"There's no need to be a little smartass."

"But it is *our* money!" I shout.

"Yes, and I'm looking after it for you."

"Yes, Ronald. I'm sure Mum would be really impressed that you're looking after us by doing absolutely *nothing*!"

And then all I hear is a dial tone.

June 1984

It's time to go through Mum and Dad's stuff. I wish we could just leave it all where it is forever, but apparently that's not healthy. When I first heard someone say that, I thought they meant that's it's unhygienic to leave stuff lying around untouched, gathering dust and mold. Now I know it's for mental health.

I don't want to do it, and my stupid tooth is aching more than ever. But it's what's done, apparently. You go through all the dead person's stuff and throw it away, give it to charity, or keep it for memory's sake. I wonder how many people who shop at thrift stores know they're wearing dead people's clothes or drinking out of dead people's cups.

At first Tracy said I couldn't be involved, so I went to Chris. "I need to be part of this. I need to say goodbye to their stuff too. Please make Tracy understand."

He obviously did, because Tracy's letting me help.

I think this could be a real bonding moment for us.

While Chris plays in the park with Trent, we're going to matter-of-factly go into my parents' bedroom and empty out the cupboards and drawers. We're going to feel nothing, just treat it like we're getting ready for a garage sale. It's just stuff, after all.

Will Mum and Dad mind? Will they think that we're forgetting about them, that we're just tossing them aside? I hope they understand. Seeing their things is just too depressing, too much of a reminder. But what will happen without a reminder? Will I just forget them completely? I'll forget how they smelled even if I keep some clothes and don't wash them. Smells fade just like everything else. Dad's shirt smells like me now. I'll forget their voices, unless I can find Mum's tapes from her tarot lady. But Dad's voice and laugh are gone forever. No tapes of him.

We don't have any photos of them around. We don't want reminders. It scares me whenever I see a photo. It's so hard to believe that one day they were standing and smiling (or in Mum's case not, as she hated having her photo taken) and now they're lying under the ground, mouths and eyes closed. Never to walk and talk and smile again.

We start with Mum's dressing table.

Tracy loves Mum's jewelry, so she takes it. I get one plain gold ring, but I'm not really into rings and things. I want Mum's books, especially the one with the yellow cover, *I'm OK—You're OK*. It's been in her room for as long as I can remember. Maybe it will help me be okay. I wonder if she read it.

It's hard to decide what to keep and what to give away, but we get out the green garbage bags and give most of it away. I keep some of Mum's crystal ring holders (Tracy doesn't want these) and trinket jars and other dressing-table things even though I hate them. They're ugly, but Mum loved them, and they remind me of that part of her. The part that wanted to be better, more.

I want to be better and more too.

Then it comes to the drawers. My pink birth card is in one, saying I weighed nine pounds three ounces. What a fat baby! It doesn't say the time I was born or anything, so now I guess I'll never know. I'll never be able to have a thorough tarot reading like Mum, and that bugs me. I wish I could find her tapes.

Now the closets. Tracy does Mum's and I do Dad's. Tracy's not too interested in Dad's stuff.

We pull out Mum and Dad's clothes and put them into garbage bags. Now Tracy and I are both sobbing.

It takes hours to go through everything, because we look at things and cry as we go. It's nice that we're doing this together. I'm happy Tracy's crying. I know it's bad for her that she never cries, so this is a breakthrough.

All the stuff we don't want, but do want, but have to get rid of, is in green garbage bags lined up against the bedroom wall. They look like a row of body bags.

Chris is going to take them to the thrift store when he gets home. I don't want to see him carrying them out to the car. It's so final. Their bedroom looks so empty. Every trace of them is gone. We've just cleaned the slate, wiped them from our lives.

Will they forgive us?

Does it matter?

Tracy and Chris are moving into Mum and Dad's room. Tracy never did get around to decorating her living room/bedroom all white the way she was going to after Trent was born. It doesn't make sense for them to sleep in there anymore when there's an empty bedroom in the house.

"Don't you feel weird sleeping in there?" I ask Tracy after they move in.

"Of course I do, but it's stupid not to use it. We have to get on with things. I'm tired of worrying what Mum and Dad would think. They left *us*. Remember?"

July 1984

Merril's her name, fixing my head is her game. Or should I say "shrinking" my head? I hope she leaves me with a little bit. She's the school counselor. The administration thought it might be a good idea for me to see her. I'm not getting any better, you see. If anything, I'm getting worse. That seems to be the general consensus.

Ha! The grief handbooks are wrong! Are they written by someone who has been through grief, or someone who studied it in school and then studied others crying on a couch?

"Oh, she's a textbook case." They'd love to be able to say that.

Merril's not like that. Don't ask me why, but I just

know. She's petite. A little taller than me, with a tiny frame but long limbs. Her slightly tanned hands are long and thin with big plump, juicy veins. I don't know why, but I love looking at her hands. Her dark hair is cut in a short pixie style.

You don't mess with Merril. I knew it the first time I saw her, before I was the kind of girl who went to the school counselor. I thought you only saw her if you were swearing, taking drugs, not doing your schoolwork, or just generally being bad. No direction? Go and see Merril. Told the home economics teacher she can stick her butter up her butt? You must have problems. Go and see Merril.

I used to walk past her office and wonder who was in there, what were they talking about. Was she being cruel to be kind, or was she just kind of cruel behind that closed fake-wood-grain door? Then she'd walk out with the guilty party and you could tell she was the boss. Girls who could tell off a teacher at the drop of a hat would shrink in her presence. I don't know what she did, but it worked.

I've now been seeing her a couple of times a week for a month. I begged the school not to tell Tracy, and they haven't. I think they know I'll stop going if they do. Tracy hates my speaking to anyone about our life. Julie said she heard Merril talking to a teacher about Tracy's being too controlling. Tracy does like to control everything. It drives me crazy, but I know it's her way of trying to keep everything together.

I've asked Merril what to do about our relationship, and she says I have to be more patient.

"Try and imagine being in her position."

"I know, Merril. I feel so guilty all the time."

"There's no need to feel guilty, just try and understand. And your little brother . . . remember, Erin, he never even really knew your parents."

"Yeah, I know. That seems so unfair."

"It's unfair for all of you. But think of it like this: you don't have all that responsibility, and you had the chance to get to know your mum and dad."

She's right. Why can't I work out this stuff for myself?

They've been good to me here at school. I know all the ladies in the front office rather intimately. They still let me come and go as I please without late notes and permission-to-leave-early slips and all that.

I have to ignore the bells when I'm with Merril. Sometimes I'm in there for "as long as it takes."

Today is going to be one of those days. She's decided it's time I relive the night of the accident. That going through it all over again will lessen the pain. Like the more you use an eraser, the less there is; each time, a little bit gets rubbed off and blown away. I wonder, though. I think an eraser is at its best when it's new. Once you start using it, it gets all distorted and dirty and becomes a funny shape and you can never get it quite right again.

"Well, we'll just rub away and see what happens," Merril says.

I suppose I've got nothing to lose at this stage. She calls the office and asks that they not disturb us. "Just relax, Erin. This will be hard, but it'll be good for you. I promise I won't let you go too far."

"I don't think I can get this upset in front of anyone. It's embarrassing."

"You should know by now not to feel that way with me," she says. She puts her long, soft hand on my dry, scaly one. I wish I'd brought my hand cream. God, what an idiot.

She starts talking in a hushed tone. "Close your eyes, Erin. Deep breaths. You're sitting at home, waiting for your parents. They're late, you're starting to get worried. What happens next? Keep your eyes closed."

It's working. I'm in the living room doing my tapestry . . . and then everything rushes back.

When I'm finished, I'm lying on the floor in Merril's office. I can't even remember everything I just said. Did she hypnotize me?

"How do you feel?" she asks.

"Isn't it obvious?" I want to say, but I just smile meekly and say I feel good.

This is a lie. I feel worse than ever. The more you relive something, the easier it gets? That's bullshit. It just wears you down. At least my toothache has gone. Weird.

*　　*　　*

I want to live like Sylvia Plath. Sylvia was the real thing.

I want to be institutionalized so I can just lie around and do nothing but be crazy. I want to lie in a bed in a row of beds filled with other girls as fucked-up as I am. We can all lie there at night under our blue and white striped cotton blankets after lights-out and I'll read *The Bell Jar* with a flashlight. We can smoke cigarettes and not give a damn who smells them on us. We'll only see the psychiatrist if we're allowed to smoke in his office, and they'll let us because we're all so screwed up we absolutely must see him once a day. He's a busy man with a touch of sex appeal. He'll like me the most because I'll come out a winner, he can see it in my eyes. He can tell I'm smart and tough. The kind of girl nothing will beat. I'm the special one. The others are just girls with no future. They'll leave here and take drugs and fuck their tattooed boyfriends and wind up jobless with three kids, if they haven't killed themselves first. But me, I'm special. I didn't do this to myself, this happened to me. That will make him love me.

Merril's told me about a place for girls with problems. They live there while sorting out their lives. It's called Rivendell. I like the name; it sounds like something out of a great novel.

We're going there to visit this week. I don't want to tell Tracy, but Merril says I have to.

"How would you feel about me going to stay somewhere

else for a while . . . a place where I can get some help for all my crying and stuff?"

The answer? "Do whatever you want."

So I am.

When we get to Rivendell, it's exactly as I dreamed. The building is dark, old red brick and looks just like the place Sylvia Plath stayed in real life. Important. We walk up the long concrete sidewalk, just like in *The Bell Jar.* I'm definitely going to fit right in here. Inside it's all thick, dark wood banisters and doorways.

The first room they take us to is one of the girls' dorms. My fantasy is real. All the beds are lined up in a row. The only differences are that the blankets on the beds are pale green, not blue, and the beds are wooden, not metal. Next to each bed are cupboards to stash books and diaries. I want to live here so badly.

I try not to smile too much in the hope that I'll look like a good candidate. As we walk, a woman asks me stupid questions, which I answer as solemnly as possible.

"Would you like to live here? . . . Why? . . . What's home like?"

Next they take me to the head administrator's office so she can ask me more questions. So what was all that about? Did I waste my solemnness on a nurse? Oh well, at least it was a good warm-up.

I'm disappointed. She doesn't have a couch I can lie on either. Does any psychiatrist in the real world have one? It's the least they could do for us loonies.

"So, Erin, do you like our facilities?"

"Oh yes, very much," I say, trying to make sure I sound as bad as I feel.

"Would you like to stay here for a while?"

"Yes, I think it would do me good."

"Why?"

"Well, I recognize that I need help. My parents died eight months ago and I'm not improving. I seem to be getting worse."

"Why do you say that?"

"Well, you know all those grief books and stuff? They say I should be at a certain stage and I'm not. It's all getting worse, not better."

"But what do you think we could do for you?"

"I don't know. Maybe . . . um . . ."

"What's it like at home? You have an older sister and a younger brother, is that right?"

"Yes. I can't stand to be at home. My sister and I don't get along. I think it would be easier for her, and she'd be happier, if I were out of the picture. I'm a burden. And my little brother . . . well, I think I'm a bad influence on him because I'm so unhappy all the time. I want to kill myself a lot and I just can't cope anymore. I think I'm going nuts."

"You're not going nuts, Erin. This is all very normal," she replies.

There. She said it. Normal. Why does everyone think this is normal? This is nothing like normal. What do I have to do to make people see that? My friends don't have any trouble with it, for God's sake, so why do these idiots? She's supposed to be a professional, but even she doesn't get it. None of this is normal. Just because people die every day doesn't mean it feels normal. It's not like I simply scuffed my knee!

"Can I come to Rivendell?" I ask.

"It takes time. First we have to review your case."

I'm sitting right in front of you. What's looking at a folder about me going to do?

"Now I'd like to speak privately with Merril."

I give it one last shot as I leave. I can feel the tears coming, so I just let them. But I don't want to appear sad. I want to seem traumatized, not just plain old sad. Sad's too simple, it's easy to fix. I want more than that. I want to be complicated and complex. Sad is just the tip of the iceberg. Sad is the one thing people can deal with. Maybe that's why it's the one thing they focus on. I need her to see more.

So I beg. It's pathetic, but I don't know what else to do. "Please let me stay here. I need this so badly. More than anything. I think I might kill myself." That gets the tears flowing. If she doesn't buy this, then she's the one who should be institutionalized.

"I feel Rivendell can help me. Please."

"Don't worry, Erin. We'll do what is best for you." I walk out sobbing, but these tears don't feel as hot and real as they normally do. What's going on? When I see Merril, I grab her hand. "Please tell her how much you think I should come here."

But it doesn't help.

I'm not going to Rivendell. Funny how what people think is best for you never is.

"Sorry, Erin, I really thought it was perfect for you, but they don't think you're a bad enough case to warrant it," Merril explains to me in her office the next day.

I'm not screwed up enough? How much more fucking screwed up do I have to feel?

"What do I have to do to be a bad enough case? Kill myself? Break the law? Burn the fucking school down?"

Merril narrows her eyes at me. "Don't say things like that, Erin."

Now I'm sobbing like an idiot. Why didn't I cry like this at Rivendell?

What am I going to do?

I hate this life.

Because Rivendell didn't work out, Merril thinks it's time I changed schools.

"Nobody will know anything about you. You'll be able to start fresh."

She seems to be implying that I'm using everyone's knowledge to my benefit. She's kind of right. I have been using the sympathy thing a bit lately. Hell, if people want to do stuff for me or let me get away with shit, then why shouldn't I let them?

"You've got to stop coming and going from school as you please," Merril says.

"But I'm doing okay. I study at home, and my grades are still good."

"Yes, but not as good as they could be," she says.

She also thinks I should stop seeing Mrs. Stockbridge at lunchtime. She's organized a special meeting with Mrs. C-J and Mrs. Stockbridge. I can tell Mrs. C-J and Merril are looking forward to it, but Mrs. Stockbridge and I are dreading it.

It's set for lunchtime on Friday. Probably so we can "go away and think about it over the weekend." That's a Merrilism.

I never realized how tiny Merril's office is. It's usually just her and me and the brown carpet, brown desk, brown chairs, and filing cabinets. I hate that it has no windows. Add two more people and it's like being squashed in an elevator.

We're all in here trying hard not to let our knees touch. Merril begins. "Who did you have lunch with Monday?"

"Mrs. Stockbridge," I answer.

"And the day after that and the day after that and the day after that?"

"Mrs. Stockbridge."

"Don't you both feel you've become too close?" Merril asks.

"Erin needs a friend she can trust, and that's what I'm being to her," Mrs. Stockbridge says angrily.

I love Mrs. Stockbridge. She's the only adult I don't pretend with. She understands the way no other adult does. Sometimes I like to pretend I'm the only person in the world for her. We just click. I wish everyone else would just go away.

I say something and Merril turns and says to Mrs. C-J, "Very Youngian, don't you think?"

I have no idea what they're talking about, but I'm nodding anyway. They start going on about how Young says this about consciousness and Young says that about dreams, and I'm nodding as if I know what the hell they're talking about. I know it's something intellectual, because their voices have shifted to la-di-da intellectual mode. I feel uneducated and stupid. I hate when I don't know something I should.

Mrs. Stockbridge seems to know, and for some reason she's growing even more angry. "Now, back to Erin, the reason we're all here," she says firmly, and they stop with the Young talk.

So the adults keep talking and all that is resolved is that Mrs. Stockbridge and I should see less of each other. No more lunchtime chats.

"Okay," we both say on the way out.

In a way I feel closer to Mrs. Stockbridge than ever. It feels like it's us against them. I don't know what's wrong with someone's helping me as much as Mrs. Stockbridge is.

"I know this is stupid, but who's Young?" I ask Mrs. Stockbridge later that day when I get to science class. I'm early. I wanted to see what she really thought of the meeting.

"They were talking above your head on purpose. God, that makes me mad! Carl Jung, *J-U-N-G,* is a famous psychoanalyst with certain theories about dreams and co-incidence and other things. No one your age knows, or needs to know, who he is."

"What's he got to do with me?"

"For the purpose of today, absolutely nothing!"

I've never seen her this angry.

"Oh, Erin, it really wasn't about you, they were show-ing off with each other. Merril isn't even a real psycholo-gist. She's a bloody school counselor!"

I'm shocked. Merril isn't even qualified to "take me back in time"? She isn't even qualified to talk to me?

I'm an experiment! A practice subject! A lab rat! I thought they were above all that at their ages. Why do Mrs. C-J and Merril need to show off? Maybe they're the ones who need counseling.

"Mrs. Stockbridge, can I still come and talk to you at lunchtime and stuff? I understand if I can't."

"Of course you can. I enjoy our chats too, you know. We'll just have to be very quiet about it. Okay?" She smiles.

"Okay."

August 1984

Ronald just called to tell us that he and Peter are moving. They've both got job opportunities in Western Australia. That's the other side of the country.

They're moving to Kalgoorlie, an opal- and gold-mining town. Maybe that's why Ronald wanted Dad's gold-panning machine.

I call Peter. "I thought you liked the job you've got," I say.

"I do, but it's time for something different."

"Can't you please stay and get something different not so far away?"

"If you went any further you'd end up in the ocean," I feel like saying.

"Don't worry, we'll still just be a phone call away, just like we are now," Peter says.

I don't understand this of Peter. Ronald, maybe, but not Peter. What's happened to him? He was always so sweet and caring. I guess it's all just too much for him.

So they're off. No party, no farewell, they just go and that's that.

Maybe they need to get away from all the sadness. They lost their dad when they were younger, then their mother, and now their sister.

That's one more than I've lost.

We all have to get up in social studies class and tell an interesting story. It can be about absolutely anything, our teacher says, as long as it holds the class's attention.

Lisa's the first to get up, as she says she's got a story we'll all love. It's about her dad's job. I really like Lisa. She's a rebel in her own quiet way. I wish I had a bit of what she's got.

"My dad works at a funeral parlor doing up the corpses. He makes up the dead bodies for viewings," Lisa says, standing at the front of the class.

Do I want to hear this?

"He gets bodies ready for funerals. First they wheel them in on a table, all bloated and hard. And get this— my dad cuts into their stomachs to let the gases out, and it stinks like you wouldn't believe."

People grimace, wrinkling their noses.

"I'm not joking. It's disgusting. And this yellow stuff oozes out of them and sometimes he has to pull the intestines out."

I feel queasy. I don't want to know this stuff, but I don't want to make a scene either. I can't run out of the room, plus I don't know that I want to. Part of me is curious. I've heard that a person's hair and nails keep growing after they're dead. I wonder if that happened to Mum and Dad.

But are these people complete morons? Both of my parents just got cut up like this. Don't they think that maybe this is just a little creepy for me? I can't believe my teacher is letting her go on. Maybe they've forgotten or they think I'm over it by now. People seem to think this grief thing is something you "get over" quickly.

I'm trying to act fascinated like everyone else, but it's not quite the same.

Lisa continues. "After that they get the makeover. Especially if there's going to be an open casket. Their skin is always gray or white, so he has to paint their faces skin color again. The skin is tight, so it's easy. Then he has to add color to the cheeks. I did that on a body while I was there. It was fun."

"Didn't it make you sick?" someone asks.

"No, they all joke and laugh about it while they're doing it. It's just like painting a doll."

Great. My parents were buried as Barbie and Ken Vincent.

"They put lipstick on the men, too, to make their lips look alive again. Sometimes they have to sew their lips up first so nothing oozes out of their mouths."

I'm laughing and oohing, but I can't take much more of this. It's so insensitive.

People just don't get it.

"Oh, and you know how some people put jewelry and stuff in the coffins of their loved ones? Well, they shouldn't, because it gets stolen." Lisa stops for a moment. "Well, my dad would never do that, but he knows people who do."

Mum's ring and Nanny's bracelet aren't there with her? Some blue eye shadow–wearing funeral parlor beautician has them on her thieving hands?

Lisa lowers her voice. "Even the clothes don't always make it on the dead people. A man who works with Dad has some pretty nice suits from dead guys."

The whole class is engrossed and I'm just grossed out.

So Mum's in the casket naked? How awful death must have been for her. Her body which she tried so hard to hide in life, totally exposed and humiliated in death. Oh, Lisa, this is all so entertaining. What a fine public speaker you make. And what a great choice of topic for this crowd. You've really worked the room.

I try to tell myself it's only their bodies. People say it's the spirit that's important. It's just so hard to detach myself from their bodies. Bodies are what we love and see and hug every day. I love you because I see you there.

The body does matter. The body is what the soul's wrapped up in. When I think of my parents, I don't think of misty spirits flying through the air. I think of what they looked like. Their eyes, their noses, their hair, their hands, their bodies.

I feel like I have neither—no body, no spirit. No signs from above, no visitations. Mum was into that otherworldly stuff, so why doesn't she give me a sign? Hey, Mum, if you're there, just come and make a candle flicker.

No answered prayers. Can you believe I still try when I feel really desperate?

So don't tell me how they were destroyed, cut open, prodded, and painted. Don't tell me her body wasn't sacred. We all like to believe that it is.

Sure, the girls are all laughing, but I'll bet they won't be laughing when their husband dies in a plane crash or their child drowns in a pool.

Because these things can happen to anyone.

Mrs. Stockbridge is leaving Beverly Hills Girls' High. She's not meant to tell me the reason, but we're closer than that.

"They suggested very strongly that I leave because you and I have gotten too close," she says at lunchtime. We're sitting in her lab.

"That's none of their business!" I yell.

I refused to go to a different school, so they're sending her instead.

"I've gone against student-teacher policy and they don't like it. Technically, they're right. I've done the wrong thing."

"What, it's a crime to be a caring person? You've been there for me. I wouldn't have gotten this far without you."

I'm trying not to cry. Being my friend is turning out to be a bad thing. She's been at the school much longer than I have. It's not fair.

"You've helped me too, Erin. But I'm a teacher and I'm not meant to get so close to students."

"I'm so sorry. It's my fault," I cry.

"It's not your fault. I knew what I was doing. It's going to be miserable if I stay . . . they'll make it that way. I'm going to miss you so much. I love you like family, you know that."

She loves me? My heart feels the warmest it's felt since the accident, and the source of the feeling is about to be taken away from me. I know she's a mother figure and I know what the psychologists would say about that being unhealthy, but what's wrong with having someone to lean on, to care about me? She's a teacher and I'm a student. So what? If I met her anywhere else, it would be okay to be friends.

I hate that they can do this. But really, I suppose I also hate that she's not my mother, she's my teacher.

Well, not even that for much longer.

It's hard loving people.

* * *

I wish I didn't love Trent as much as I do. I'm so scared of losing him that I can't stop taking photos of him.

"Trent, pick up the phone." I've lifted him up and put him on one of Dad's barstools.

"Pretend you're speaking to someone."

And he does. He looks so grown-up. As grown-up as a three-foot-tall person can.

I help him get down.

"Hey, Trent, put these on."

I'm dressing Trent up to look like a little man. He's wearing a gray tracksuit, tan Ugg boots, and Mum's big sixties-style sunglasses.

His face is dirty from playing outside. It's perfect. He looks like he has stubble around his tiny, pointy chin.

"Now sit on the sofa with this can of beer."

I feel bad for using him like this, but we're both giggling uncontrollably, so I know he's loving this too. "Now give me a thumbs-up."

And *snap,* I've got it.

Trent the man.

I've just come home from a rotten day at school. Mrs. Stockbridge has only been gone a few days and I'm miserable. To add to my misery, I just went out to put the trash in the backyard only to discover that Chris has bought a dog. He's always wanted one and couldn't have one when he lived at home with his parents, so now we're stuck with it. A great big German shepherd. Shouldn't we all have discussed it first?

In two days, our beautiful yard, Dad's pride and joy, has turned to shit.

The dog keeps tipping the trash can over, tearing up the bags, and throwing garbage all over the place. It's so dirty and depressing, especially now that it's winter. Dirty diapers, torn paper, and food scraps wet with dog saliva cover the grass. I've picked it all up a few times now, and I've had enough. The grass is so long that you can't see the dog poop hiding in it until you've stepped on it. I wish I never had to go out there, but I have to hang my washing on the line (because the dryer is too expensive to run), which the dog then proceeds to tear down. I have to make sure my clothes don't actually hang where the dog can reach them. And the pool is a mess. There's so much green stuff floating on the surface of the water, you can't see the bottom. Even the big lemon tree out back has given up. All the lemons have fallen to the ground.

The dog won't stop barking. He's just torn up all the rubbish again and has my jeans in his mouth. Chris won't do anything to stop him because he doesn't think it's a big deal. When I ask him to do something, he just says that's what pups do. In other words, *Just deal with it, Erin.* After seeing his family's messy yard, I understand why he doesn't care.

"Stop barking!" I yell at the dog through the sliding glass door that leads to the backyard. "Be quiet!"

I'll just tap the door lightly with my bare foot and see

if that scares him into silence. The glass wobbles slightly and he keeps barking at me.

"Stop it, stop it, stop it, please!" I feel like one of those mothers who scream for their baby to stop crying before they shake it to death.

"I hate you!" Now I feel like a crazy person. "Stop it!"

Crash!

Shit! I didn't think I could do that. I've just put my foot through the glass door and it's shattered. And now the dog's running into the house . . . not exactly what I had in mind. What am I going to do? Tracy and Chris are going to kill me!

Too bad I didn't kill myself with a shard of glass going through the wrong vein. Then they'd feel really bad about the dog ruining my life. But all I've done is get a few cuts. God, I'm an idiot. I've just made everything worse.

"Come here, you stupid motherfucker of a dog."

I've got to get him out of here, but how? Now he's going to tear everything up inside the house as well as outside.

The car's just pulled up in the driveway. Tracy, Chris, and Trent are home.

"Tracy, I'm so, so sorry. The dog was barking like crazy and I got so mad I kicked not realizing the door was closed"—what a liar—"it was so clean"—what a brown-noser—"and it smashed everywhere."

Tracy's just glaring at me.

Trent is standing too close to the glass, so I quickly pick him up and tell him to play in his room for a while so he doesn't get hurt.

I run back out and Chris is calm but angry. He puts the dog in the garage, where he gets some wood to make a barrier in the doorway.

I start to pick up the glass.

"Oh, Erin, just get lost, will you?" Tracy screams.

"But I did it. I want to fix it."

"You're going to get cut," she says, looking like she's going to stab me with one of the pieces of glass. "Just go to your room."

Then Chris comes back in and glares at me. He tells me the same thing.

I walk away and grab the phone, sneaking around the corner where they can't see me. I call and beg Ronald for some of our money to pay for the glass. I haven't tried the begging thing with him yet.

"Please, Ronald. Please. Tracy and Chris are furious. This would help things a lot."

"What the hell were you doing kicking a door in?" Ronald says.

"I was just so frustrated and upset."

"Well, you'll just have to live with it, won't you?"

"You don't think living without Mum and Dad is enough? I have to suffer more because you won't give us our own goddamned money! God, Ronald. When did you become such an asshole?"

He hangs up and I'm on a roll. I walk back out to the scene of the crime.

"Tracy, don't be so stubborn. Let me help. I can pay for it with extra shifts at Cookie Man."

"No, Erin, forget it. It's over now."

"No, it's not, and you know it."

"What do you mean by that?" she says through gritted teeth.

"I could solve all of this by paying for it, but you won't let me."

"Yeah, because it will take you weeks to make the money and it needs to be fixed today! I'll deal with it the way I do everything else."

And with that she walks away.

The window repairman comes and asks how it happened. When I tell him, he laughs. It's funny how something can seem so bad to one person and like no big deal to another. He makes me feel better.

Until I turn and see Tracy standing with her arms folded.

September 1984

School feels so empty without Mrs. Stockbridge.

My other teachers keep their distance from me. *"Wait! Calm down,"* I want to say. *"I don't want you to be my mother."* It's not like I'm looking for any old mother figure. That would be pathetic. I had a mother, thank you very much! I'm discriminating; I don't get close to just anyone. Mrs. Stockbridge and I clicked. That doesn't mean I'm going to cling to any female of mothering age. Give me some credit, please.

I do advanced modern history, where it's just Julie, me, and the teacher, and things are different now. It used to be that we'd laugh and chat, eat scones and sip tea, but now it's all business. I suppose I don't blame the teachers for pulling away. They don't want to be forced to leave the school.

I miss Mrs. Stockbridge. There's no one to talk to. I hate bothering my friends with all this crap. It's not something they should have to hear.

"Why don't you talk to me?" Tracy says one night out of the blue.

We're in the kitchen and she's slamming drawers shut.

Despite the Tracyspeak, this is great. She must finally want to *talk* talk. I knew it would happen sooner or later when I least expected it. Some people just take longer than others.

I'm so happy I don't care how much noise she's making with the cupboards. I know she's only doing that because she's nervous. This will be so good for her. She won't be so angry once she talks about things. She's bottling it all up, Merril says.

"Well? Why don't you talk to me?" she repeats.

"Because you've never wanted to talk before. I've tried," I say.

"I don't understand why you don't talk to me instead of talking to that bloody science teacher of yours!"

What? This isn't how it's meant to go. I'm frozen to the spot.

"She's not even at my school anymore. Anyway, how do you know about her?"

"I don't know exactly, I just heard it somewhere."

"Where?"

"Well, you know, you seem so pissed off. I needed to know what was going on with you, so I found your diary and read it."

I can feel the blood rushing from my cheeks. "You read my diary? How could you?"

Yes, I have a secret diary. . . . Well, not secret anymore.

"I read it for *you*," she says.

"Oh yeah, what were you going to do? Actually read it, then talk to me, the way I always beg you to?" I want to say. *"Oh, you care so much, that's why you read it. That's why you searched all my drawers to find it. If you cared so much, you'd* talk *to me instead of being* angry *with me the whole time. You care? You did it for me? Bullshit!"*

I can't believe this is happening. *"You're just nosy and want to know how I feel about you. It's all about you. Tracy, Tracy, Tracy."*

Why can't I say any of this to her? Why am I so scared of her?

"Tracy, why didn't you just ask me what was wrong?" I ask instead. I'm not going to cry. "We could help each other through this. We could be such great sisters if only we talked. Please, Tracy. It's not healthy this way. It's getting ridiculous. No one understands better than us what each of us is feeling."

Okay, so now I'm crying . . . just a little.

"You fucking idiot, talking to a fucking stranger about our life!" Tracy spits out. "It's pathetic. You should keep this stuff to yourself."

"I'm sorry, Tracy, but I needed to talk to someone."

"You can talk to me!" she snaps.

"Every time I try to talk, you get angry and stop me or walk away."

"Look, Erin, this is our private business. You think some teacher gives a shit about what you have to say? You think she cares?" She's fuming.

I've never thought about it that way before. She's right. I've been talking to a teacher who probably deep down isn't the slightest bit interested. She probably used to go home to her husband and rave on about this stupid girl who wouldn't leave her alone.

No. Would she?

Oh God. Am I a needy, pathetic loser?

"So you really hate me that much, do you?" Tracy asks, looking angry and hurt.

"It's just a diary," I mutter. "It doesn't mean anything."

"Yeah, right," she says, walking away.

I follow her out to the back room. "Tracy, I don't really mean what's in there. I just get so frustrated that we never talk about Mum and Dad or how we feel or anything."

"Look, forget about it. I know how you feel now," she says, not looking at me.

"Tracy, please. I don't want us to go on like this. It's awful. We shouldn't be this way."

"Forget it, Erin. Just go to your room like you always do."

I feel terrible that Tracy's seen my diary. Now she's

hurt when she didn't have to be. That's the point of a diary, isn't it? To get stuff off your chest that you don't really mean—or if you do mean it, it's stuff you would never tell people because it would hurt them. I hate Tracy sometimes, but I don't want to hurt her. Probably because I do understand her and the way she is. She can be a bitch sometimes, but that's because she's so angry and unhappy. I know she can't help it. She's stuck with me and Trent. Her life is ruined.

Everything's going to be different from now on. I can feel it. Tracy and I have just had a breakthrough. Maybe the diary discovery was a good thing.

We were on our way to Auntie Connie's for lunch when we started fighting politely.

"You want me to be your mother, and I'm trying. But I just can't do it," she says out of nowhere.

I stare at her. "What makes you think that?"

"Because that's what you want."

"I've never said that. I hate that you try to be a mother to me. It drives me up the wall."

We're on Auntie Connie's verandah. For once Tracy's almost crying. And now I am, as usual. No great shock there.

"Just be my sister. That's all I want," I say. Suddenly it all makes sense.

"All this time I thought you wanted me to be Mum." Her voice cracks. "That's why I get so angry. I just can't do everything."

"I don't expect you to. I just want you to be my sister!" I tell her. "Tracy, we can be a team."

We hug. We actually hug. It's awkward, but we actually do it. Tracy and I are touching each other. It feels weird but great. It's a true *Days of Our Lives* moment, except there's no bad music, unless of course you count the Greek music wafting from inside through the white wire-screen door.

"All I want is for us to talk and share stuff the way sisters are supposed to. We can help each other get through this, Tracy."

We're smiling at each other. It's like something has changed, like things might be different after this. We'll do more things together. We'll be friends. We'll bond, because that's what tragedy ultimately does. It brings people together.

"I'll try. I promise I'll try," Tracy says.

I smile. "Me too."

It's been a week. It isn't working. She tries to smile and be nice, but it's like she can't help herself when she looks at me. It's like she can't stand to be in the same room as me. What is it about me that makes her look at me that way?

Maybe it's something in her subconscious that she doesn't even know about. Or maybe it's nothing like that. Maybe it's that she still has to sign parental guidance forms for me from school. You're not my mother, Tracy, but you have to pretend to be because I'm a minor. I hate how at school they say, "Take this home and get a parent to sign it." What about all the little kids in the world who don't have any parents? There are a lot of us, I'm sure. I think I'll ask the school if I can sign my own forms from now on.

Anyway, I'm not giving up. Things don't happen overnight.

"Auntie Connie, I don't know what to do." I've walked up to her house after school to get away from ours. Tracy is angry and I'm not sure why. "No matter what I do, Tracy acts like she hates me."

"Erin, you have to try and be more understanding. She's under a lot of pressure. She's had to become a parent to you and Trent overnight."

"But I don't *want* her to be a parent to me!"

Now I'm crying and Trent's just come over and hugged me, which makes me cry more. I brought him with me because he loves going to Auntie Connie's place.

"Why are you sad, Erin?" he asks.

I tell him I hurt my foot, so he bends down and rubs it before running back to Peter's room.

"So what do I do?"

"Try and imagine what it's like for Tracy."

"But I do . . . all the time."

"In a way, you're better off than both Trent and Tracy."

"How?"

"Well, you don't have the responsibility, and think—

you at least had your parents for as long as you did. Trent probably won't have any memories."

I know what she's saying is true. Merril said the same thing. But at the same time, I'm furious. This isn't a picnic for me, either!

Mum always said I was impatient. Maybe people never change. I sure know I need to.

My London style has grown out and I need a haircut. I don't want to ask Tracy, but she'll be hurt if I go to anyone else. And it's not like we can afford a fancy salon anyway.

I'm on the kitchen chair wearing her plastic cape and Trent is sitting on the floor coloring.

"Erin, turn your head to the left." Before I have a chance she's got my head between her hands, turning it for me.

"Turn right." Grab! *Snap!*

"Put your head down." Push!

Ouch! Did my nose just touch my chest?

I look down at Trent. He's drawing what looks like me in a cape.

"Move your head to the right"—and if I don't do it quickly enough or far enough—shove!—she does it for me.

We talk about my hairstyle. I tell her what I want.

Tracy tsk-tsks. "Oh, you can't have that. Your hair's too thin. It will just fall flat."

"Well, what about this?" I say, holding my hair up to show how short I'd go.

"No, your face is too chubby."

"Well, you know best. Just do what you think."

So she cuts and I sit there terrified as my head almost gets ripped off. Despite all that, she does do a good job. I have to admit, she is a really great hairdresser. If only she had a better chairside manner.

October 23, 1984

It's been twelve months already, so why aren't I over it?

The books say that at three months I'll feel this and at six months that and at eight months this. . . .

Books on grief make it all seem so serenely sad. Like you're walking around in a silent, fluffy cloud of dull pain. But it's not really like that. Grief comes up behind you and hits you over the head. There are no angels playing harps in the background, no soft sunsets or fields of flowers blowing in the breeze.

See that person whose mother or husband or child has just died? They look sad and somber, don't they? Tired? Depressed? Calm? Don't be fooled. On the inside they're probably screaming. You just don't see it.

I feel like I've been skinned alive. All red and moist and raw. One bump and I'll be in agony, unable to do anything. I can't be the only one who feels this.

The Five Stages of Grief
1. Denial
2. Anger
3. Bargaining
4. Depression
5. Acceptance

One, two, three, four, and five, you're there. *Bang! You're cured.*

Bang! You're dead is more like it.

And don't forget, all grievers out there are supposedly the same. Taking the same simple steps, on the same sad timetable. You're not special, just another bereaved. *Bereaved.* What a bullshit roundabout word.

Bereaved: greatly saddened.

Sad? Sad is when you say goodbye at the airport, not at a gravesite.

Books on grief think they cover everything, but they can't even get their own covers right. Pretty white flowers on pale pink and yellow backgrounds, beautiful warm orange sunsets. Why are orphans like Annie, Pippi Longstocking, and Oliver always singing and having adventurous lives? *Don't forget you're just a drop in the ocean—this too will wash away.* That was on one of our stupid sympathy cards.

The books dance around the issue, gloss over it. They don't tell the brutal, intricate truth. They forget to mention that grief is full of unimaginable terror and horror. They make grief seem soft and gentle. Pastel and breezy.

Grief's not like that. Grief's got balls.

I may be imagining things, but I think people at school and my boss at the Cookie Man are becoming impatient with me. It's like when I was on the Shopfront tour. I act really happy, but I think they can tell that there's more, and it annoys them or something.

"Come on, Erin, it's been three months!" ". . . six months!" ". . . a whole year!" They've seen too many movies where the parent dies, the kid cries and feels sad for a while, and then life resumes as before and the sun shines brightly.

Grief is different for everyone. Look at Tracy and me. How much more different could we be, and we're grieving for the same people. It's been twelve months and she still won't talk about our parents or the accident.

At least, not to me.

One year, and sometimes I actually feel worse than I did eleven months ago.

I've decided to turn my pain into art. I'm going to photograph the five stages of grief using my hands as my subject. Julie's helping me. We're using black-and-white film, for that timeless look.

It's early morning. We're in my now perpetually messy backyard. Oh well, great artists are usually poor and have to work with their crummy surroundings, I tell myself.

"Take my photo, Erin." Trent has just walked out in his checkered flannel bathrobe and slippers. He looks like a little Hugh Hefner.

I shake my head. But he looks so cute with his long eyelashes and short thick hair that I give in.

"Trent, come inside! It's freezing out there," Tracy calls a few minutes later from the kitchen window.

I've told Tracy I'm doing a school assignment. She'd think I'm crazy if she knew what I'm really doing.

Trent grins at me and Julie and runs inside.

Julie and I are set up for our shoot. I drape red fabric over a kitchen chair to give it a theatrical look. The camera's on a tripod I borrowed from school. I focus the lens on the chair.

"Are you *sure* this isn't stupid?" I ask Julie one last time.

She tucks her brown curls behind her ears. "It's not. Now just shut up and do it."

I kneel beside the chair and plunk my hand in the seat. I'm holding the phone. Julie is behind the camera. "Yes, that looks good," she tells me. "That's great. Perfect! A little to the right."

I clear my throat. "Okay, I'll start with the October twenty-third phone call."

Frame 1: I'm holding the phone in anticipation.

Frame 2: I'm gripping the phone tightly (you can see by my knuckles).

Frame 3: I've dropped the phone on the chair and my hand is open and tensed like it's saying *aaaaah!*

"Do you think that looks like the night of October twenty-third?" I ask Julie. I've told her a bit about it, so I trust her judgment. She nods.

"The next frame should be shock," I say.

I let myself go, I'm really feeling it. My hand's doing a jittery, spastic movement to represent my shaking that night.

"Now!" I say at the peak of my feeling.

"That's weird, but I think it definitely expresses some kind of pain," Julie tells me, checking the camera.

"Now the 'fuck you, up yours' shot. I think I'll just stick up my middle finger, what do you think?"

"That just about says it," Julie answers, and we both start laughing.

We spend the next couple of hours capturing the stages of grief. Of course, there end up being more than five. You can't put grief into five categories. But I didn't expect more than twenty! If the stages are real, then I'm a very jumbled griever. I've jumped from one to two, back to one, two, up to three, back to two, to three, two, one, two, one, one, two, four, one, three, two, four . . . but never five. Not yet, anyway.

By the time we're done it's getting dark. Julie and I are

so tired we pack up and go inside and make a chocolate cake and eat all the batter before we even get a chance to put it in the oven. We do that a lot these days when she comes over . . . I suppose because we can.

Yes, there are some advantages to this grief thing.

It's two days later and I've got my photos back. When I see the pictures of Trent, I feel like a real photographer. But then I look at the grief photos. They're a joke. I'm a joke. I'm no artist. What was I thinking? They don't express anything. They just look like I placed a dismembered hand on a chair. In my "Shock" picture my stunned hand looks like Thing from *The Addams Family*. In my "Death" shot, I look like a hand model doing a skin-care commercial. My "Suicide" picture is particularly stupid. My limp hand is lying there on the chair, holding an open bottle with pills falling out, like in a tragic movie where the heroine tries to kill herself. It might have worked, except the bottle of pills that are meant to symbolize killing myself are *vitamins*! I didn't realize the label would show in the photograph! I can hear the minister now. . . . *"We are here today to celebrate the life and mourn the passing of our dear sister and friend Erin Vincent, whose young body was riddled with that merciless killer, vitamin C."*

I don't even want to show them to Julie. But of course she asks to see them. We lay them out on my bedspread.

"They're good," she says, picking one up and studying it.

"Come on, I can tell you're just saying that," I say, crossing my arms. "You're a terrible liar, Julie."

She shrugs. "Well, they're unique."

"That's like telling an ugly person they have a great personality."

Julie laughs. "Okay, they're weird. But think of all the great artists who were mocked in their own time and when they died everyone loved them."

"Well, there's something to look forward to," I say, laughing too. I carefully put the photos back in the envelope.

Mrs. C-J has offered to take me to see Mum and Dad. That's how she put it.

"Would you like to go and visit your mum and dad?" she asks.

"They're dead. Remember?"

"You know what I mean. Would you like to visit their grave? I'd be more than happy to take you."

"It's hours away, you know."

"That's fine."

Do I really want to go and see where they're buried now that it's all closed up? Do I want to go back there? People always do; you see it in movies all the time. "Um, I don't know."

She tells me the offer's always there if I want to take her up on it. And then I decide I will. I ask Tracy if she wants to come, but she says she's never going back there.

Mrs. C-J and I take a day off school. I love that I can

do things like this . . . and with a teacher! I feel kind of special.

She comes to the house to pick me up. Mrs. C-J has brought along shovels and gloves and stuff.

"What's all that for?" I ask. Visions of her making me dig them up so I can really believe they're dead fill my head.

She tells me that people always bring gardening tools to keep their loved ones' graves nice.

"Would you like to get some flowers on the way?" she asks.

"I don't know. Should I?"

"Well, I think it would be nice."

It feels kind of sappy to me, but we get some anyway at a roadside stand. Kind of like the fruit stand Mum and Dad were crossing to that night, but I keep this to myself.

We drive up to the cemetery and it looks just like it did on the days of the funerals. Dry and sunny.

We get out of the car and pull the gardening tools from the trunk. I know exactly where the graves are, but for some reason I pretend I don't.

"I'm not exactly sure where they are," I call over my shoulder. I walk in the opposite direction of their graves, which are on the edge of the hill.

"Here they are, Erin!" yells Mrs. C-J. I don't know if yelling in a graveyard is okay, but we're the only ones here in this small country cemetery, so it's probably fine.

"Oh yeah, that's right. I remember now," I say, trying

to act surprised. It's weird that Nanny's grave is next to theirs. Who would've thought you could visit a grave and end up buried beside it two weeks later?

I look, but don't really look, at the headstones, and then Mrs. C-J and I clean up all the weeds and dead flowers. I wonder if anyone else has ever been to visit their graves. I feel nothing.

When we're done, she says, "I'm just going to leave you to have some time to yourself, Erin."

I shake my head. "That's okay. I don't need it."

"Still, I think you should, and I need some shade."

So she walks back to her station wagon and I sit on the edge of the grave. I know I should cry, but all I feel is sick to my stomach. I'm probably supposed to talk to them, but I'm not about to start talking to a rock.

What would I say anyway? *"Hi, how's heaven? Are you in heaven or are you just a bunch of nothing under there? So, Mum and Dad. Why did you leave? It's bad enough for Tracy and me, but what about Trent? How could you?"*

If you want to speak to your dead parents, I don't think a cemetery is the place. It's where their bodies are perishing, rotting away, with worms crawling through their eye sockets. Gross. If there's one place in the world where my mother and father aren't, it's here. If they are floating around, I doubt they'd hang around some boring old gray headstone, living it up with all the other decayed bodies. I don't understand this whole graveyard thing. It's just an ugly gray rectangular rock sticking up from the ground, surrounded by a bunch of smaller rocks . . . and now my stupid yellow flowers. It's awful.

"Well, I know you're not here, but I love you. Bye."

And we pack up the car and drive away.

I'm not going again. My parents aren't there. It's just rocks with their names on it. That's not them.

I've decided there is no God. So why am I opening the Bible? This stupid white leather Bible Mum gave me years ago?

"Oh, thanks, Mum, it's beautiful. I'll read it every day."

What a big fat liar I was. I tried to read it, but it was a bit boring with all the *thee*s and *thou*s. But still, here I sit. Flipping the gold-edged pages like some loser who can't handle things.

Mrs. C-J mentioned something in scripture class today, and I'm curious. I suppose it's no different than looking in one of my history books about slavery in the United States or foot binding in China. I like to educate myself. I want to make something of my life. You don't experience something as big as your parents' dying and not feel an urge to make something of yourself. I don't want to be one of those kids who have something bad happen and then they go down the tubes and end up in the gutter on drugs with scraggly hair and black circles under their eyes. What would be the point of all this suffering if I end up a big fat nothing?

So *that's* why I'm checking out the Bible. It's just another book, really. It's considered great literature in some circles. Full of great stories: murder, revenge, sex, adultery, brothers killing brothers, women turning into salt . . .

Anyway, Mrs. C-J said there was something in the Bible I might like.

"Erin, you should take a look at Job—I think it may be of interest to you."

Job's miserable, but he wasn't always that way. Job had a happy family and a successful business. Then one day Satan says to God, "I'll bet if you take away all his riches, all he has, he won't be faithful to you. He only loves you because his life is so good." So God says, "I can prove to you how much Job loves me. You do whatever you like to him, make him suffer all you want, and I'll bet he still loves me and not you."

Place your bets, place your bets!

So Satan kills Job's family, covers him with boils, and makes him poor, and Job says to God, "What the fuck?"

"I lie down and try to rest; I look for relief from my pain. But you, you terrify me with dreams; you send me visions and nightmares" (Job 7:13–14).

So even old tough farmer Job could've used a sleeping tablet or two. Sometimes I can't sleep without the pills the doctor gave Tracy and me. They're smooth and shiny pale yellow.

Job did the pretend smile bit too. "If I smile and try to forget my pain, all my suffering comes back to haunt me" (Job 9:27–28). Maybe there are lots of people walking around with fake smiles covering up sad hearts.

Then God talks directly to Job. Why did God speak to people back then and not now? Hey, God, when are you going to have a chat with me?

"Who are you to question my wisdom with your ignorant, empty words?" (Job 38:2)

Oops! Did he just hear me?

"Have you any idea how big the world is? . . . Answer me if you know. I am sure you can, because you're old and were there when the world was made!" (Job 38:18, 21)

Whoa! God is sarcastic! God goes on to tell Job that he helps people who are suffering and that suffering isn't for nothing. Hmmm, wasn't Job's suffering just a game God was playing to prove a point?

At the end of the story, even though Job's life is restored, his family is still dead and the suffering is still within him, part of him. You can't take that back, God.

God says we learn from pain and become better people because of it.

I don't think I'm becoming a better person. I'm becoming a girl with a bad attitude.

At least I don't have boils.

First the Bible, now this: I'm going on a Christian retreat, and I'm not even one of the converted. Actually, I just want to go away to the mountains for the weekend, and if I have to listen to some sermons and singing, that's okay with me. No one has to know if I'm not listening. I'll just lift my head to the heavens every now and then and smile that mindless Christian smile and no one will know the difference.

"I'm so glad you're coming, Erin," Mrs. C-J says when I tell her I'll be joining her and the six other girls from school.

Megan is coming, so at least I'll have one of my friends there. Ever since Megan's mother ran out on her, her dad, and her brother a few months ago, Megan's become interested in God.

"It's so hard. I feel like my mum's died too," she said to me last week when I was at her house.

That really made me mad. I know her mother left, but Megan can still visit her any time she wants. Well, maybe not any time. I get the feeling her mother doesn't want her around too much. I suppose that's almost the same as not having one. But Megan doesn't have to lie in bed at night and imagine her mother's body rotting away. I suppose she might imagine her mother in bed with that other man.

Is that worse?

Megan is nervous about leaving her dad for the weekend. "What if he gets depressed while I'm gone?" I think it will be good for him not to see Megan for a couple of days. With her bobbed red hair and petite frame, Megan looks just like her mother.

"You can call him from up there," I tell her.

So we're off to a cottage in the Blue Mountains for the

weekend. Apparently they're called that because at different times of the day the trees look blue.

It's a Godfest with workshops, music, and food. And lots of gatherings. At our first one, Megan and I sit on seats facing a large outdoor wooden stage, under a tent. We sing a few songs. A preacher gets up and talks. I mostly zone out.

"If anyone sitting here today feels the desire to give their life to God, please come to the front now," he says. Part of me would love to go up there as a joke. But I don't want to make Megan mad.

A woman begins playing an organ, and people start running to the front. Some of them are crying. Some of them are falling down. A few of them are twitching. Then I hear people murmuring around me. It sounds like pig Latin, and half the tent is speaking it.

"Mrs. C-J, what's happening?" I whisper.

"They're speaking in tongues. It's direct from God."

"Do they know what they're saying?"

"Not really, but it's God's language."

Poor God, he can't even speak properly. No wonder he never talks to anyone anymore. No one would understand him.

The newly converted walk back to their seats, some crying but all still looking the same. Maybe it takes a while to work.

"Now a final prayer before we go out into the world and spread God's love on this glorious day," the preacher says in a hush into his microphone. Heads bow. Mine doesn't. I'm watching out for God . . . or something . . . anything.

Nothing.

I can't blame him. I wouldn't be in a hurry to come and play this crowd if I were him. I'm sure he doesn't like all this stuff either. He probably finds it as strange as I do. If he exists, that is.

"Well, what did you think of that, girls?" Mrs. C-J asks as we file out.

We all say it was great, but I wonder how many of us believe it.

We all pitch in and help make dinner that night. It's exciting being in a house with six other girls. There's lots of fun and laughs, but I can't stop thinking about the day. I'm still so angry inside. I guess I'm just like most teens. Isn't that our shtick?

After a Saturday-morning hike we have another gathering, where I sit feeling even more pissed off with God and all the weirdos there, and two workshops about Jesus and sin before going back to the cottage and packing up for the train ride home.

"Well, girls, I want to know what each of you thought," Mrs. C-J says once we're on the train. Everyone tells her it was great. I'm tempted to talk in "God's language," but Megan seems into the retreat, and I don't want to act like I'm not.

* * *

I do want to believe in God even though I don't want to. I want to go to church even though I hate church. I want to pray to God even though he's not really there. I want him to help me even though he hurt me. I want him to hear me even though he's deaf.

I don't want to be some needy dork who speaks in tongues and can't cope without God and all that crap, but sometimes I think maybe God does have a greater plan for me. For Job. For everyone. What doesn't kill us makes us stronger, blah, blah, blah.

There's a church within walking distance of my house. I've now gone there a couple of times with Megan, and it all seems pretty normal. Everyone's young. There's no weird tongue-talking in this church. I still think singing hymns is pretty stupid, but whatever. I try to ignore the tambourine and triangle. But I'm not quite convinced yet. I'm not going that easily. I wouldn't jump out of a plane with a parachute on my back before reading up on it, and I'm not about to jump into this without some solid proof.

I've read about the Dead Sea Scrolls (the for and against); I've read about Jesus, and you at least can't deny that he lived; I've read and read and read the Bible. Now I've just got to have faith.

I'm starting to feel like I can't do this on my own any-more. I don't want to use God as a crutch, but the days aren't getting any better and I'm not getting any better. Trying God out for a while couldn't hurt, could it? I can stop whenever I want. It's not like God's a drug I won't be able to give up. You get hooked on heroin or coke. You don't get hooked on God.

My mother believed in God, and it didn't seem to turn her into a mindless idiot. Dad thought it was all pretty stupid. I wonder what he would think of me now.

November 1984

 got up in church today and "gave my life to God." Can I get it back if I want?

God's not as bad as I thought. It's the world that's all screwy.

I like liking God. It takes so much less effort than hating him. It keeps me busy too. There's fellowship on Friday nights, church on Sunday, and other events during the week. Oh, and I'm learning to play the guitar. It's fun. Trent dances around my room while I strum the guitar I borrowed from church. He's too little to know my playing sucks.

With God hovering around I'm never lonely, never alone in my room late at night when I can't sleep.

Tracy thinks it's hilarious that I've started listening to Christian rock music. But I don't care. It's all hopeful and triumphant. It makes you want to jump up and accept your Academy Award, fly like a bird, shout to the rooftops.

Amy Grant's my favorite singer. I figure if someone that pretty can be a Christian, then it can't be all bad. Christianity isn't just for ugly losers who can't get a date and people who can't cope with life.

Keith Green is a great Christian singer too. He died in a plane crash. I wonder why God would kill off someone like that. It seems pretty stupid. Like having an important letter you want to send but you kill the mailman.

It's funny, but I still can't imagine my parents in heaven with God. I don't think I believe in heaven. I never imagine seeing them again when I die. I don't imagine them up there looking down on me. I believe in heaven for other people, but I don't think Mum and Dad are there. They're nowhere.

I just got home from school.

Chris is crying. This terrifies me. "Chris, are you okay?" I ask.

"Erin?" Tracy nods toward my room and walks in that direction. I follow.

"What happened?" I ask.

"Katrina's dead."

Katrina? Chris's sister? "What? How?"

Tracy winces. "Hit by a train."

Chris had to go and identify her, and apparently she was so messed up no one else in his family could handle it. Maybe they think he's a death expert now.

Katrina was on a train, twirling around the poles you hold on to, and stuck her head out the window when it was coming to a tunnel. Who would think pole dancing could kill you? I wonder if her head came off. I still seem to have morbid thoughts like that. I must pray more.

I wonder what Chris had to identify. He doesn't say anything about it, and I don't want to ask. He wasn't that close to Katrina, but I imagine it will scar him for life.

Although her brother and my sister are an item, Katrina and I didn't talk much. She was cooler and tougher than I am, and she was always doing stupid stuff. She scared me sometimes in school, before I knew her as Chris's sister, because she was one of the tough girls. On the outside, anyway.

I feel bad for judging her. Funny how you don't feel bad about it until someone's dead.

Katrina did whatever she wanted. She didn't let her family know where she was half the time. She was a wild child.

It's been two weeks since Katrina died, and Chris is trying hard to be strong. He walks around looking like he's about to cry but never does—at least, not in front of me.

Chris's mother seems to be loving the attention. She's

been on the news. When reporters knocked on her door, she invited them in with refreshments at the ready.

I don't feel for her the way I thought I would as a fellow griever. I know I said everyone grieves differently, but you'd swear she was hardly grieving at all.

I suppose I don't really know what goes on in her private moments, the way nobody knows about mine. Maybe everyone's saying, *"Look at Erin, she sure smiles a lot! She mustn't care."*

I can't believe I'm so judgmental, thinking about Chris's mother the way people have probably thought about me.

I guess I'm not that different after all.

December 1984

It's Christmas again. It's not so bad now that I'm a Christian. Grandma and Grandpa arrive for breakfast, and like a good Christian I just smile and try to be loving, even though they are telling Tracy and me we're not doing the best thing for Trent. Thank God we hardly ever see them these days.

When they leave, we head off to Chris's parents. This time it's more for them than for us. This year we're doing the cooking and looking after them. It's the same as last Christmas but with different grievers. It's actually good to have to think about other people. Just like last year, Trent cheers everyone up with his endless chatter about his exciting new toys.

January 1985

"Now I want you to look at that chair and pretend it's your mother. Talk to her."

It's six p.m. and I'm in the cold, concrete church basement with the new youth leader, Dave.

"I think I can help you," he said last Sunday at church.

I feel like I'm in a bad acting class and the pressure is on to give a show, a good performance.

I'm his little project, I know that. He does care, though. He's a former bad boy who found God and now tells us to stay away from alcohol and drugs. That's easy to say when you've already had the fun of trying them, but he's a cool guy. He's really nice, and easy to be around.

And he's a good poster boy for Christianity, with his dark, messy hair and baggy pants and surf shirts.

"Now, Erin, look at the chair and pretend it's your mother."

"Ever tried pretending your mother was a chair?" I retort.

It's not easy, especially when it's a rickety old spindly wooden chair. If my mum were a chair, she'd be a plush, soft, dusty pink velvet chair with big armrests and sturdy legs. The kind of chair you never want to get out of. It's insulting to see her as this piece of cheap junk. She'd be most offended.

"I can't do it. I'm sorry."

"Well . . . imagine your *father* is the chair."

Gee, couldn't we use a different chair this time? Dad would be a black leather chair with studs at the back. The leather would be warm and worn but the studs would be cold on your back. You could get comfortable in it, but not quite.

"Sorry, Dave. I have to at least use a different chair."

So Dad gets to be an ugly green vinyl chair with a tiny layer of padding on the seat.

"Dad, I'm so angry with you," I say in a monotone.

"Oh, Erin," Dave says, laughing, "that was pathetic. Put some heart into it."

I know Dave wants to help, and I like the attention he's giving me, but I feel like an idiot talking to a chair in an empty church hall with a young Christian surfer watching me. I eventually work up to tears and drama, but I feel so exposed and stupid and I don't even know if I'm being real or if I'm just doing it for him. Is my theater training just kicking in? Errol would be impressed with this performance. But those playacting days are over now. Once the tour ended, I stopped going to Shopfront. I didn't want to go back to the scene of the crime, where I'd had that terrible thought, and my heart just wasn't in it anymore. Now I can't even bear to go past on the train.

Dave is studying to be a counselor, and I think I may be his first project. Quite lucky, getting a girl with dead parents at your first parish. What an opportunity.

I have to save Tracy while there's still time.

We're in the living room. Chris is out front teaching Trent how to kick a soccer ball.

"But Tracy," I say, "you'll end up with big red boils growing all over your body. They'll get all juicy and infected and yellow pus will ooze out like a volcano." I have to tell her to change her ways before she dies a horrible death or the world ends, whichever comes first. Hopefully the world will end first. I can't stand her most of the time, but I don't want her to die, especially not before me.

"Tracy, promise me you'll stop having sex with Chris. God will forgive you if you stop now. Promise me you won't do it anymore. Because if you do, you really will be covered in boils. Even on your face," I add for extra shock value.

That should get her. Looks are important to Tracy, and boils are not going to be in fashion anytime soon.

"If you don't stop sinning, even worse things than that will happen. You'll die and go to hell, and hell is worse than what we've been through. You'll end up in a place full of other people with oozing boils and red raw flesh hanging off their bones. They'll all gather around you and scream and moan and try to touch you because you're new to hell and all your skin is still intact."

I can't believe she's actually listening to me and not walking out of the room. This is a first.

"Don't be stupid, Erin," Tracy tells me. She gestures around us. "Hell is here and now. I'm already living in it."

"It won't matter that you've suffered here on earth. God won't care that your parents have died. None of that will matter if you keep on sinning and don't pray to God to save you. They told us all about it in fellowship last night."

"You're crazy. What are they doing to you at that church?" She's laughing, she's actually laughing for the first time in a long time. But why does it have to be about this?

"Tracy, this is serious, you've got to listen to me!"

"Hey. Don't worry about my soul, okay? I don't think God's going to punish me for something so stupid when he's made me suffer so bloody much in this life here on earth."

"But Tracy—"

"Shut up, Erin." She walks outside to join Chris.

I suppose I'll just have to keep praying for her.

✳　　✳　　✳

At church there's this gorgeous guy, the minister's son, but he doesn't even know I exist. He's got dark curly hair and blue eyes and is a really good guitarist. I think about him all the time. Even though it's frustrating, I'm kind of glad I have these thoughts, otherwise I'd think there was something wrong with me. You see, every guy who's interested in kissing me is highly unappealing.

There's Phillip Sidebottom—the name says it all. He sits behind me in church. I can almost feel his hot lusty breath, and when the minister talks about death or losing someone you love, Phillip always puts his hand on my shoulder.

"Piss off, buster!" I want to say, but as usual, I just sit there like a big dummy while the sweat from his clammy hand runs down my shoulder. Then when the service is over and people get up to leave, Phillip comes up to me with this pathetic "I'm a sensitive guy" look on his face.

"I know this must be so hard for you, Erin. I'm here for you one hundred percent."

Why is it that I always get the dorks? It makes me angry that whenever a dorky guy at church is interested in me, he uses the accident and my "pain" to try and get close. It's disgusting. I didn't think this kind of thing would happen in the house of the Lord. Aren't Christian boys supposed to be nicer than non-Christian boys?

And Phillip isn't even a boy—he's twenty-three, which makes him doubly disgusting.

Eventually Phillip sees he's getting nowhere and gives up. But then with Phillip out of the way, greasy Mark

Bean, cream of the loser crop, starts in. He doesn't even try anything different. He sits behind me and goes through the same motions as Phillip. But Mark's worse. He's almost a bit scary. He follows me around, leaves me notes. And, he's twenty-four.

Why are guys in their twenties interested in me? I'll tell you why. Because they think in my sad and sorry state I'm a sucker for anything.

I may be sad. But I'm not a moron.

I'm a pretty light sleeper now that the stupid doctor won't let me have any more sleeping pills. He doesn't want me to be addicted. Doctors, what do they know?

I'm lying in bed. It's just after one a.m. and I can't sleep. Then I hear a noise. Something's going on outside our house. I get out of bed and walk out to the living room.

The sound's getting louder. I look out the front living room window.

"Oh, Erin, I'm here for you;
Oh, Erin, don't be one, let's be two."

Mark Bean is walking around the cul-de-sac, strumming his guitar and singing. He's serenading me. How embarrassing! What if someone else in the street hears his moans?

I sneak out onto the verandah.

"Mark, what are you doing?" I whisper-yell, so that he, but nobody else, can hear me.

He smiles like a lunatic. "Just listen," he says before strumming the guitar again.

"Shhh! You'll wake up the whole street," I hiss. I can't believe Tracy hasn't heard him. But he doesn't stop.

> "We're made for each other—
> Can't you see?
> I care for you so much.
> Like the wind loves the trees."

"Listen, Mark, I need some sleep. You'd better go home. It's really nice of you, though." Why am I always so damn polite to these idiots?

He's just standing there looking at me like "What?" I go back inside.

He starts singing again. Now I'm really creeped out. I don't know what to do. I suppose I'll just lie in bed and wait for him to get bored and give up. I can't decide how furious I am because I'm starting to feel bad for him even though he scares me.

Now I really need a sleeping pill.

"Please don't do that!" I yell.

It's a week after the midnight serenade. Mark has sneaked into the garage to get to Dad's lawn mower and is now mowing our front lawn at a million miles an hour.

"Mark, stop it! Please." I run outside as soon as I hear the noise. It's seven a.m. Sunday. Our neighbors are going to hate us.

"I want to do it," he pants.

"Yes, but I don't want you to. This isn't helping, Mark." I cross my arms over my chest and go back into the house. This is the second time he's done this.

Tracy's up. "I'm getting a bit worried about this guy," she says to Chris as he walks, yawning, into the kitchen. "He's twenty-four years old, for God's sake. What's he doing chasing a fifteen-year-old girl?"

"Yeah! And you know what's coming?" I say, thrilled that Tracy cares. "Next he's going to kill me, cut me up into little pieces and store me in his freezer so we'll always be together." I'm joking, but I'm not.

"Oh, Erin, don't be ridiculous," Chris says. But he hasn't really seen Mark in action.

For once, Tracy takes my side. "I think she's right; he's getting worse. He was here the other day, mowing the lawn like an out-of-control maniac."

Why is Tracy so concerned? I don't get it, but I like it. If someone from outside the family treats me badly, the people inside get all protective and caring. . . . Interesting.

Come and get me, boys!

I wrinkle my nose. "Yeah, and the other night he was outside serenading me."

"What?" Tracy is appalled. "You should have told me, Erin. What was he doing exactly?"

"Oh, you know, strumming his guitar and singing on the front lawn. It was pretty creepy."

"I'll go and speak to him, but I think you're overreacting. He's just trying to be nice," Chris says in a deep, stern head-of-the-household voice.

Ever since I got angry at his dog and kicked the glass door in, Chris has been different with me. He thinks I'm a big overreactor, and I guess sometimes he's right . . . but not this time.

I don't know much about sex. Mum never had a birds-and-bees talk with me. What little I know came from a bad movie.

Beverly Hills Girls' High decided that age twelve was time for girls to learn about the things that go on between a man and a woman. Like we don't already know, we all said to each other. Actually, I didn't dare tell anyone, but at the age of twelve I didn't really know as much as the other girls seemed to.

"On Monday we're going to watch a film about love and sexual intercourse," my personal development teacher had said.

I figured it was going to be a bit racy, because we had to take a permission slip home for our parents to sign. I wondered what the big deal was. Mum let me watch R-rated movies, especially ones she thought would enrich my life. So Mum said nothing and signed mine.

The big day came. I sat in the dark next to Julie,

waiting for the movie to start. It was times like these that I was glad there were no boys at our school.

The lights went out, the movie started, and I soon decided I was never having sex. I didn't want to end up red and raw with pus oozing out all over the place. And that was just one of the things that could happen. You could get crabs. Imagine having little crabs like at the beach running all over you down there! Then there are warts, which I thought you only got on your fingers, blood, smells, and pain, pain, pain. Then there's the baby factor. But still, that's nothing compared to warts and painful peeing. I couldn't believe how messy it all was. It made me wonder why people do it at all.

It was not what I imagined when I lay in bed listening to love songs. I thought we were going to see a film with men and women holding hands and kissing, getting romantic in the moonlight and then doing the deed with soft moans and declarations of love. Not ugly striped sheets stained with yellow pus!

No wonder I'm still scared of the whole thing.

Despite the weirdos, Megan and I are starting to think a lot more about guys. Julie couldn't care less. If a normal boy ever showed any interest in us, we wouldn't know what to do. Being at an all-girls' school doesn't help matters. There's the neighboring Narwee Boys' High, but we never really mix with them. So, unlike most people, we don't even know how to talk to boys like normal human beings. Luckily, there's a handful of boys at church who are musical, surfer types who don't look Christiany in the slightest.

They probably think Megan and I are the church dorks!

Neither of us has ever kissed anyone. We're completely abnormal for our age. Dead parents and runaway mothers tend to take your mind off such trivial matters. But all of a sudden it doesn't feel trivial. It's time for action.

We decide to practice on each other. It's a bit crazy and lesbian-like, but what other choice do we have? I'm sitting on Megan's blue carpet, my eyes are closed, and I'm heading toward her—that's if she hasn't chickened out and snuck out of the room. I peek. She's still there.

She peeks too. And then we start laughing. We can't stop.

So much for practicing.

I'm celebrating my birthday this year with a party. I still think birthdays are meaningless without parents, but maybe it's time to try and see how it feels. You don't turn sixteen every day, I guess.

It's a hot, windless Saturday night and all my friends from church are in the backyard, which is clean for once. The dog is at a friend of Chris's.

Apart from Megan, no one from school is here. I'm going to the movies and lunch tomorrow with Julie and my other friends because I know they would feel uncomfortable here and I'd be embarrassed. Julie hates the whole Christian thing but doesn't give me a hard time about it.

So it's just church friends for tonight. Some are huddled around a fire, some are playing guitars and singing, some are dangling their feet in the pool, and others are inside listening to music.

Chris is manning the barbecue with some of his mates, and Tracy is in the kitchen with a couple of her friends drinking champagne, watching us and laughing. It's great to see her laugh even if it is at me. That's what big sisters do, right? Laugh at their dorky little sisters.

No one's swimming, even though the pool's sparkling clean. Chris spent days getting it ready for tonight. I walk around with Trent holding my hand. He's so cute. I love showing him off to people.

"Hi, everyone." I smile at the group huddled in a circle. They're engrossed in a serious spiritual discussion.

"Happy birthday, Erin," they say, not quite in unison, before going back to their conversation.

I sit down with Trent on my lap and try to join in, but it's clear I'm not going to be able to contribute much. Megan's standing by the pool talking to one of the cuter boys, and I don't want to interrupt them. Trent runs off to Chris and the barbecue.

I'm starting to feel out of place at my own party. Was this just an excuse for people to come to a big gathering and eat free sausages? And to top it all off, Mark Bean is sitting in the shadows strumming his guitar and staring at me. Chris said I had to invite him—I couldn't invite everyone from church except him.

Thank goodness Julie isn't here. She'd be mortified, with all the religious singing and stuff.

I have to get away from Mark.

"Hi, everyone!" I yell over the music as I walk through the sliding glass door into the house.

"Hi, Erin," a boy named Martin says, heading my way. I'm not really into Martin, but lately he's been really nice. Plus he's the only person at my party really talking to me.

"Hey, birthday girl, let's sit down," he says. "You have a lot of great albums."

"Thanks," I say as we sit on Mum's brown floral sofa.

He puts his arm around me, which doesn't feel right, but I just go with it. I wish I could see past his buck teeth, red hair, and freckles.

Maybe I have to learn to be more open to all types of boys.

Martin's moving in. He's getting closer. His teeth are coming at me as if he's about to nibble me like a carrot.

I don't want to be sweet sixteen and never been kissed. If it has to be Martin, so be it.

We have several awkward attempts. At first his teeth hit mine. I keep instinctively closing my mouth. I feel like he's coming in from all different angles. Finally, we kiss, and it's pretty gross. I want to run and hide in the bathroom and puke.

Martin smiles. "We just need more practice," he almost hisses through the gap in his front teeth.

"Yeah, I guess," I say like a pathetic spineless jerk who is so desperate to get this kissing thing over with that she'll risk having her teeth knocked out.

"We need to be alone where we can relax."

"Maybe, but this is my party," I say, making it clear that I won't go off alone at my own party. Not that anyone would notice. But that's my excuse to Martin and I'm sticking with it.

"Well . . . how about we try going out? Then we can practice all we want."

"Um . . . okay," I say like a dork.

It doesn't make sense. He grosses me out. So why have I just agreed to be his girlfriend? What am I doing? Have I not gained any balls from all my suffering and torment?

I'll bet Tracy never had this trouble when she was sixteen.

God, what a party! I can't wait till it's over.

February 1985

Megan's been teaching me how to sew. I've finally made something I'm proud of. It's a jacket made out of kids' curtain fabric. It's very colorful, with lions and tigers and elephants, set against a jungle background.

I wear it today to church. During the sermon, the minister starts talking about how we present ourselves to God, how what we wear shows how much we respect him, how showy clothes are a sign of ego. And he's looking right at me! And, I realize, so are some other people.

I feel stupid and self-conscious. As we file out after the service, the minister looks at me meaningfully. "I hope you especially got a lot out of my sermon."

When I get home, I take my stupid jacket off and throw it on the floor. I thought Christians were meant to be accepting of everyone, no matter what. It's about what's on the inside, right? He had no right to say that. It's not like I turned up at church in my undies! If it's okay for a kid's bedroom window, I think God can handle it.

I make an effort to look good. God probably *likes* my creativity. I'm sure God doesn't care what I wear to church.

So I pick up my jacket and hang it up.

I don't want to go back to that stupid church. It sucks! It's got nothing to do with God anyway. Who needs judgmental Christians and creepy boys? Goodbye, Martin.

What was I thinking in the first place?

Church numbed me, distracted me. It helped me ignore what was really going on. A diversion, the same way a hobby keeps people from thinking about things they don't want to think about.

The next Sunday Tracy asks me why I'm not going to church and I tell her I'm done with all that Christian bullshit.

"It's about time you came to your senses," she said.

"Yeah. Sorry for being such a weirdo with all that hell stuff."

I have just read *The Diary of Anne Frank*. Suffering? I have nothing on Anne Frank. I'm just a middle-class white girl living in a nice neighborhood. I can come and go as I please. I am under no threat of death. I don't have to hide behind a bookcase. I can leave my bedroom whenever I want.

She suffered and never complained. She was strong and noble and wise.

She dealt with her pain beautifully, the way I should, but don't.

She was wise and I'm stupid.

She was noble and I'm pathetic.

She had no self-pity and I feel sorry for myself sometimes.

She was never too angry and I'm always too angry.

She was positive. I'm negative.

Why can't I be more like her?

The Diary of Anne Frank is full of love and hopeful things and little stories and Anne's observations about the people around her. Anne Frank loves through it all. She had so much more to contend with. I wish I had her courage.

She's a hero.

If my diary were published, it would be called *The Diary of a Whining Crybaby*. Mine wasn't written with eloquent prose. My diary is full of bad writing and dumb metaphors and mean things about Tracy. Fuck this and fuck that. That person's an asshole and I'm pissed off.

I burn my diary.

Something I must remember: no matter how bad things get, there's always someone worse off.

Like I could go out and meet someone who lost their

mother and their father plus one other family member. I'm not starving. I can go to school. I'm not hiding behind a bookcase. I have hope, the possibility for a better life. I know my parents loved me, so I don't have any of those "my parents don't care" hang-ups. Not like the girls at school who you can tell don't feel loved at all.

There are a lot of people worse off than me:

1. Tracy, because she's the oldest.
2. Trent, because he never really knew our parents.
3. Starving Africans with bloated bellies and nothing in them.
4. People in war-torn countries dodging bullets and bombs.
5. Kids whose parents don't love them.
6. Little orphans (the real thing) living in homes.
7. Street kids.
8. Abused kids.
9. Poor people.
10. Paraplegics.
11. Quadriplegics.
12. People in iron lungs.
13. People dying of cancer, especially kids.
14. People with deformities.
15. Mental patients.
16. Deaf people.
17. Dumb people.
18. Blind people.
19. Deaf, dumb, and blind people.

20. Retarded people.
21. Homeless people.
22. People in prison who aren't guilty.
23. Kids who have lost not only their parents, but their whole family.

Then there are all the people I've learned about in my modern history class—peasants in tsarist Russia, all the Jews in the Holocaust, black slaves in America, Chinese women with tiny bound feet . . . the list goes on and on.

I don't feel so bad when I think about how terrible they must all have felt. I must never forget that. Maybe I should put this list on my bedroom wall.

I've got to take control of things. I've got to fix things. It's time to make some changes. There are some things I can't change, but there are others I can.

It's five a.m. on the first day of my "Have a Life That's Cool, Do Well at School" plan.

My mission (now that I have chosen to accept it): Study hard. Do brilliantly at school. Have a great career. Make some money and end our money worries. Change our lives for the better.

Plan of attack:

    5:00 a.m.: Out of bed every day.

    5:05 a.m.: Sneak a peek at Trent (for inspiration).

    5:10 a.m.: Strong coffee.

    5:20 a.m.: Sit on bed or at desk.

5:30 a.m.: Study.

8:00 a.m.: Get ready for school.

8:30 a.m.: Leave for school.

9:00 a.m.: School.

12:30 p.m.: School library during lunch-time.

3:30 p.m.: Walk home from school.

4:30 p.m.: See Trent. Play. Snack.

5:00 p.m.: Change into comfortable clothes.

5:05 p.m.: Homework.

7:00 p.m.: Dinner. Takes a while, because Trent's not that into eating, so we have to coax him and keep a close eye on him so he doesn't hide any food. It's good because it gives us something to focus on.

8:00 p.m.: More homework.

9:00 p.m.: Coffee break.

11:00 p.m.: Two NoDoz tablets.

1:00 a.m.: Bed.

Do this every day except Thursday nights and weekends, when I'm at Cookie Man.

End result: A great career and enough money for us all to have a good life without stress and worry.

Tracy's not a huge fan of my mission. "There's more to life than studying, Erin—like helping me more with the housework, for starters!"

I try to help as much as I can, but I know it's not enough. But time is precious and I have to do well at school. She'll understand one day when I'm able to pay for her and Chris to laze on a tropical island sipping cocktails while Trent and I fly off to Disneyland.

My timetable is very strict, but I do make allowances as long as they help move the plan along. Like sometimes I combine Trent and homework: he sits on the floor next to me and colors and plays with his trains. He's a constant reminder of the things I'm working for.

I have a choice. Life can be completely shit forever, or I can try and make it better. If I do well at school, any career will be open to me. The world will be my oyster. I hate oysters, but whatever.

If Anne Frank could keep on with her studies in the middle of all that tragedy, so can I.

March 1985

"Erin, what are you doing?" The strict, scary head of the science department has called me out of school assembly. She's tall and thin with short dark hair and an even shorter temper.

What on earth is she talking about?

She continues. "I've been watching you for a long time and said nothing, but it's time someone did."

What is this woman going on about? She's never spoken to me before.

"This has to stop. You look absolutely terrible. It's time you started making an effort."

I blink at her. "What?"

She sighs. "Take a good look at yourself. Your hair and

your clothes are dirty. You've been wearing that same shirt for so long now. You're an attractive girl, Erin. What are you doing to yourself?"

"I'm wearing green, aren't I?" I say defensively. I have my green workman's pants and Dad's shirt on. My rebellion is starting to get a little tired, I must admit. Besides, I'm a senior now. Seniors can wear whatever they want as long as it's bottle green on the bottom and white on top.

"Yes, but you know what I'm talking about, Erin."

"But I hate the stupid uniform. You can't force me to wear it."

"No, I can't." The official senior school uniform is a short (and the world does not need to see my fat knees) green skirt and white collared shirt. Most of the girls wear it with some sort of personal variation—a T-shirt underneath the shirt, knee socks, a sweater. "But I've heard you like to sew. Is that right?"

"Yes."

"Perhaps you can put that talent to good use." She tilted her head toward the door. "Now get back into assembly and I'll expect to see some changes very soon, Erin."

I just look at her and nod and walk back into the assembly hall to hear the school principal's boring speech about the sports carnival. In a weird way I know she's doing me a favor. I'm surprised the school hasn't said anything about my clothes before now. But she didn't have to butter it up with compliments. A pretty girl I'm not.

Do I really want to give up Dad's shirt, though? It's become a part of me.

But now that I'm getting my act together with my schoolwork, maybe it's time I took a good hard look at my appearance. It would mean I could express my style. Maybe it's a sign.

My uniforms are a hit.

There's my bohemian look: baggy green harem pants with a white T-shirt.

The 1940s Marlene Dietrich look: green below-the-knee pencil skirt and white oxford.

And my favorite, the Katharine Hepburn offscreen look: green suit pants and white sweater.

Girls and teachers have been commenting on them all week.

"Erin, I'm impressed," the science head says, winking as she passes me in the corridor.

Megan's angry, though. "I know it's not your fault, but it isn't fair. I've been sewing for years. You start and get all this attention. It's like everything."

"Everything?" Since I stopped being a Christian, we've kind of avoided each other. Her jealousy makes our friendship even more stressful.

"Well, it's always about you," she says, not meeting my gaze. "I know my mum didn't die, but it's still hard, and nobody cares because you're worse off."

I'd wear that stupid uniform my entire life if it meant

I could see my mother again. But that's not an answer you can give someone whose mother walked out on her.

Later that week I'm called into Deputy Principal Edwards's office.

"Erin, we've all been talking about your wonderful designs. We were wondering if you'd like to design a new official uniform for the senior students," Mr. Edwards says.

I know they're only doing it to make me feel useful and special, so I say no, but thanks anyway. I tell them Megan taught me to sew. "She might be interested," I tell them. I'll stick to designing just for myself.

I need a new hairstyle to complement my changing moods and fashions. Something light and cheery.

Tracy suggests I get a perm to give my limp hair some life. She's taking me to training night at the salon where she works Friday nights. Trainees practice on anyone willing, and it's free.

"They won't ruin my hair, will they?" I ask.

"No! And anyway, I'll be there to supervise and make sure they don't."

So Tracy drives me to the salon and I get assigned Tess, a four-foot-eleven trainee with a bad haircut. Not a good sign.

"So what do you want?" Tess asks nervously, biting her nails.

"A perm," I tell her, wondering if I should request someone else. But maybe I'm not even allowed to do that.

"That's perfect. I need to practice more perms," she says, putting her large black apron on.

As Tess walks away to get the rollers and solutions, I wander over to the bench where Tracy is chatting with another stylist. "Are you sure this is a good idea?" I whisper.

"Yeah, of course," she whispers back. "Stop being such a pain. Don't worry, it'll be fine. Tess knows what she's doing."

Because my sister's a hairdresser, I know that small orange rollers mean tight curls and big blue rollers mean loose curls. Hang on! Tess is using small orange ones! I look over at Tracy and make a face, and she's watching and not saying anything, so it must be all right.

Tess pours smelly perm solution over my roller-covered head.

"Now, it needs to stay in for a while, so just sit back and relax," she says before walking over to the senior hairdressers, including Tracy, who are marking them on tonight's performance.

Have my hair done and relax—I didn't know the two went together. Lovely. I'm just going to lean back, close my eyes, and enjoy this.

After thirty minutes Tess is back and ready to roll out my thicker, fuller, less limp hair. With each unroll a little bouncy curl pops out.

Five minutes later and all the rollers are out. I look like a teenage Medusa!

"Don't worry, it will look great once it's dry," Tess says in a voice trying to mask her obvious concern.

She dries it and it starts to shrink. It was supposed to be a light, wavy perm. Instead, I am sporting an Afro. A blond Afro! I look like a white black girl. No. At second glance, I'm a sheep. My shoulder-length hair has sprung up around my ears.

I try to pretend I like it. I get up from my chair and walk over to Tracy.

"I look like a fucking sheep!" I whisper so Tess won't hear. She's probably already distraught enough, knowing she fucked up so badly.

"Didn't you see what she was doing?" I say, trying not to sound accusing. "Look at me, Tracy. What am I going to do?"

"I thought it was going to be fine. She seemed to be doing the right thing to me," Tracy says, and now I officially know I must look disastrous. "I don't know what happened."

"Couldn't you see the size rollers she was using? You always tell me the smaller the rollers, the tighter the perm. She used those tiny orange ones!"

"I couldn't see the rollers."

She's acting like looking like a sheep is no big deal.

"You were right here. There are mirrors everywhere!"

"Calm down, Erin! Perms are always too tight at first," she says through gritted teeth before storming off to a scared-looking Tess on the other side of the salon, where

I was sitting earlier getting my Afro. Hey, I can see the angry look on her face perfectly well from here! Why couldn't she see my hair being tortured? Was she even watching?

It's Monday morning and I still have an Afro. I almost don't need a pillow anymore. My hair's padding enough.

I do not want to be in school. I can't make myself look even slightly better. Any other bad hairstyle you can disguise. But not this one. I've tried hair clips, but they won't stay in. A scarf is even worse—it looks like a hot-air balloon has landed on my head. I can't even wear a hat; it just sits there on top of my hair, five inches away from my scalp. So it's just me. The sheep.

"Baaahhhh . . . baaaaahhhh . . ."

I can't believe I just heard that! I thought having dead parents might exclude me from that sort of teasing in the school corridors, like I'd be off limits. But obviously nothing makes you immune to bad haircut jokes in a school full of girls.

"It's just hideous, isn't it?" I asked my friends by our lockers. They're trying not to laugh.

"It's doesn't look so *baaaad,*" Julie says, laughing halfway through her sentence. My friends all crack up. "I'm sorry, I just couldn't help it."

"Oh God, what am I going to do?"

"You could always go and have it shorn off and make a sweater out of it," Lorraine says, and I must admit it is sort of funny.

June 1985

I'm finally old enough to drive and I want to buy a car. So it's time to get some better-paying work. Goodbye, Cookie Man; hello, seafood and candlelight. I just got a job at a five-star seafood restaurant outside the mall.

"I'll pay you twelve dollars an hour and you can keep all the tips from the nights you work—your tips and mine," the tall, dark-haired Egyptian owner tells me upon giving me the job. He waits tables too sometimes.

"I don't expect to take home your tips," I say, not knowing where to look. His right eye floats, like one of those pop-out, wandering crab's eyes.

"No, if you're a good worker, you'll deserve it. This is not an easy job, you know," he says with a wink.

After about a week, he introduces his girlfriend to me, which I don't understand, as I've also met his wife. The two of them are sitting at the dark red bar. The lights are low "for atmosphere."

"Nice to meet you." I smile as sweetly as I can before slowly walking back to the kitchen, finding it difficult to move in my tight black skirt.

"Your skirt must be stylish and tight," he had emphasized when he'd hired me. "It gives the place a gourmet feel."

Doesn't the food do that, or are the customers going to eat me?

The tips are amazing! I've been working here three or four nights a week for two weeks, and it appears I'll not only have money for home, but will also have my car in no time! That's if I can stick it out.

I don't know if I'm imagining it, but I'm starting to think that the tips he gives me are to compensate for letting him squeeze past me and brush up against my butt when I'm taking orders (even though there are more open routes to the kitchen) and to entice me to join him for a meal after a hard night's work, which I always say I can't do.

Maybe it's harmless. But what about the wife/girlfriend thing? And the fact that the brushing, squeezing, and pinching are getting more frequent?

"Chris, you're a man. What do you think of this?" I

ask him one night, filling him in. He'll probably just think I'm being a drama queen.

"Erin, you can't go back there."

"What, you honestly think he'd attack me or something?"

"Trust me. You can't go back."

Damn! Damn! Damn! I knew he'd say that, because I already knew it myself. I may be stupid sometimes, but not that stupid.

So I call the restaurant the next day.

"Oh, hi. It's Erin. I won't be coming in anymore. Sorry." I hang up and that's the end of that.

Oh car, Oh car, you seem so very far. . . .

I get another job working at a pizzeria up the road owned by two Italian brothers. Joe is sweet and married, and Mick, the younger one, is single but seems nice as well. I don't think I'll have any trouble here, although the money isn't nearly as good.

It's been a month and I love it. No carrying lots of plates at once or being nice to rude rich people. I'm even learning to toss pizza dough.

"Hey, Erin, do you want a ride home after work?" Mick asks me one night. He's just bought a white muscle car, which he wants to drive everywhere.

"Yeah, sure, that would be great."

This is the third night Mick has driven me home, and he wants to sit in the car outside my house and talk for a while. The front is one long seat, and he moves in a bit closer and I almost hug my window. He's your boss, Erin, and all he said he wants to do is talk; don't jump to any conclusions.

What should we talk about? It's not like we have anything in common. He's in his late twenties, and I'm sixteen. He goes on and on about the restaurant and how well he's doing, and hey, don't I love this car? He tells me how I'm so great and he loves the way I'm always smiling and all that.

I swear, these men must be desperate. Boys my own age don't go after me—they don't even notice me. I don't get it. It's not like I'm anything special to look at.

Don't jump to conclusions, Erin.

I love this job, and we all love the pizzas I get to bring home. Tracy won't eat them because they're fattening, but Trent and Chris devour them.

It's been a week since our boring chat in the car, and Mick has taken to kneading my butt instead of the pizza dough. I almost jumped over the counter from fright the first time he did it.

I tell Joe I'm quitting one night when Mick is taking a delivery order. He looks sad. "Is it the money? We can give you a raise."

"No, really, I just can't work nights anymore."

"Well, if you ever want your job back, it will always be here."

I do want my job back, now! But your stupid loser brother is a creep—*he's* the one who should quit. But Joe and Mick are family. I'm just the hired help.

I've found the answer to the car problem.

I'm going to win one. Not just any old car, a bright yellow one with four-wheel drive. I can feel it in my bones; I'm going to be the winner of the Good Ones Car Contest. It's meant to be. All I have to do is drink as many small cartons of Good Ones, a carob and honey soy milk drink, as I can, because you can enter their contest as many times as you like. You just cut out the side panel and send it in. So it's Good Ones on the way to school, at school, on the way home from school, and at home.

Tracy and Chris can't keep driving me everywhere. They're not my parents. They hate it and I hate it, and we hate each other every time we're in a car together. I feel so dependent on them, like I have no freedom. Ronald refuses to give us money to help us pay our bills, so there's no way he'd pay for a car for me.

I'm sick of Good Ones, but I can't stop. I'm at the point where I buy Good Ones and dump them down the sink (sorry, starving people of the world), I've had that many over the past month.

I didn't win. I'll never win. I have no destiny. I have no car. I think I'm now allergic to carob and honey.

*　*　*

Grandma and Grandpa are my last hope. What a dilemma! When I think of them, I don't think of happy, hopeful things, especially when it comes to their best friend—money.

Grandma believes that once you have money, you hold on tight and don't let go. You don't put it in the bank for the government to get hold of, and you definitely don't stick it under the mattress like all the other stupid old people who are sure to be robbed. You bury it in the yard, put it behind the washing machine in a sock, or stick it in the freezer with the peas and chops.

I know it's useless, but I have to try.

I decide to ask when they come over to see Trent next. They come over every month or so for a quick visit, and it's always the same thing. Almost two years after Dad died, they still complain that we don't understand how much worse off they are for losing a son and how we're ruining Trent's life by not letting him live with them.

"You have no idea. You're lucky, you're young and have each other, but what do we have?" Grandma asks.

"Umm . . . us?" I feel like saying. They've never been all that thrilled with Tracy and me, being evil Mum's evil daughters and all.

"I'm all alone, I have nothing. Nobody cares about me. It's worse for me, you know. What about me?" Grandma cries.

"We care, Grandma, don't be silly. And what about Grandpa? You still have him. And all your nice neighbors," I say, although I know they hate my grandparents.

She eventually calms down. Grandpa is in the back-yard. I figure it's now or never. There will never be a right time.

"Grandma, I was wondering if I could ask you a favor," I say, scrunching up my face in "I know you'll hate me for asking" pain.

"What could I possibly do for you when I need help?"

"Well, you know how I can drive now? Well, I've been trying to save up for a car so Tracy and Chris don't have to drive me everywhere and also so I'll be able to drive Trent around. I still don't have enough money and was wondering if you could possibly loan me some."

"I don't have any."

She's lying. Just two weeks ago she was complaining about having an extra thirty thousand dollars she had to hide so the government wouldn't find out and stop her and Grandpa's pensions. "I think we'll buy some new leather furniture and change the guttering and maybe re-paint the front and get one of those extra-thick wire-screen doors," she'd muttered.

Maybe in her old age she's forgetting what she says and what she doesn't. Then again, she and Grandpa are the sharpest old people I know.

"They'll probably outlive us all," Mum used to say. She was right. The good die young; the horrible people of this world always survive the longest. I think their mean-ness keeps them strong.

"Grandma, I promise I'll pay it back as soon as I can."

"How much do you want?" she snaps.

"Well, I have money saved, but I need another, say, two hundred dollars."

Grimace. "I don't know if I have that much to spare," she says.

"It won't take long for me to pay it back, I swear. And just imagine—I'd be able to visit more with Trent."

This gets her thinking.

"You'll bring Trent around to see us?"

"Yes, of course."

"Maybe you could help me do my grocery shopping every week and drive me to the doctor when I need it . . . and drive me to the Veterans Club and—"

"Sure, Grandma, whatever you want."

I knew it would come at a price higher than two hundred lousy dollars. But maybe I'm seeing this all wrong. I should be positive. Maybe this is her way of trying to be close to me, to see me more. Maybe she just can't express herself well. This could be a good thing. I might get to know her as a person and actually like her.

"Yeah, and we can go out to lunch together and everything," I say.

She pauses. "I'll have to see if I can afford it."

"Okay. Let me know. We could have a nice time, Grandma."

Who am I kidding?

But I need a car.

The next day Grandma calls. "I can manage two hundred dollars, but only just, mind you. It isn't easy for me."

"Oh, Grandma, I know. Thank you so, so much. Thank Grandpa for me too. I really appreciate it."

This is fantastic! So I have to visit them and go grocery shopping and kiss Grandpa on the cheek every time I see him and drive Grandma to the doctor if she needs it. It's either that or no car.

I'm free . . . but not so free.

"So, Julie, what do you think?"

I'm parked in Julie's driveway in my new car—a little white Corolla. It's a bit of a bomb, but it was the cheapest one I could find that wasn't falling apart. At least it's tiny and cute.

"It's fantastic. Is it yours?" she asks.

"Yep, I got it today. I saw it in the paper, Chris came with me to see it, and that was that. Do you want to go for a drive?"

"Abso-bloody-lutely. Hang on, I'll just tell Mum."

She runs inside and comes straight back out with her mum, who has a tea towel over her shoulder, as usual.

"Where are you going?" she says to me, waving, or should I say flicking, the tea towel.

"Hi, Mrs. Price. Just around the block a few times."

"Well, no speeding, and wear your seat belts. I want you back here in an hour, Julie. All right? One hour."

Julie opens the creaky door and gets in.

"Isn't this fantastic? We'll be able to drive to school every day. I can pick you up in the mornings," I tell her, excited at the prospect of not catching the bus anymore.

"Umm . . . Erin, it's stick shift. I didn't think you knew how to drive manual," she observes.

"I don't."

"So how the hell did you get here?"

"Well, Tracy and Chris each gave me a disastrous lesson ages ago."

Lots of screaming, lots of cursing. But for once, it wasn't because of the accident. All of the girls at school say their parents yelled at them when teaching them to drive.

"So I'm learning as I go. I've driven here mostly in second gear." We decide to visit Megan.

Julie bounces in the seat and quickly discovers it doesn't really have much bounceability.

I'm driving in second gear and . . . *crunch* . . . third.

"Oh no, here comes a hill. I haven't done hills yet."

"Well, let's go the other way," Julie says wisely.

"Nah, how hard can it be?" I say. "I have to do it sometime."

"You're the driver," she says. "This is so great! We can go anywhere!"

I start up the hill in first gear, then second. "Shit! We've stalled."

We're rolling backward until I remember where to put my foot for the brake.

"Chris said to avoid hill starts. Apparently they're the hardest thing."

"Oh," Julie says, biting her lip.

I start the car and am in first gear. Now I just have to

slowly take my foot off the clutch, accelerate, and let go of the hand brake.

Crunch. Stall. Roll.

"Try again. You can do it." Julie's trying to act positive.

"Here comes a car behind us."

"Tough, they'll just have to go around us."

So I try again, and again, and again. And all we do is roll and stall, roll and stall.

"Shit, I can't get us off this hill. What if I can't get you home in an hour?"

I'm starting to panic and Julie starts laughing.

"Are you laughing at me or our situation?" I'm trying to join in.

"Both. And don't worry about Mum. I'll just blame you." She chuckles.

"Ha! Very funny."

I know it is kind of funny in a pathetic way, but I can't seem to de-panic.

There's an older man watering his garden about two houses up from where we are stuck. I hop out as Julie waves at the stupid honking cars behind us to go around.

I explain what's happened. "I hate to ask, but would you mind starting it and getting it to the top of the hill for me? It's silly, I know."

"No, of course not. It would be my pleasure," he says, putting his hose down.

We walk to the car and Julie climbs in the back and I sit in the passenger seat as the man patiently explains what he's doing as he does it.

"Thank you so much! I don't know what we would have done without you," I tell him as he gets out. "I'd love to drive you back home, but—"

"No," he laughs," you just keep going now. Good luck, and stay away from those hills for a while."

"Thank you!" we both yell as we drive away, avoiding anything that even vaguely looks like a slight rise in the road.

"Hi, Grandma, you ready?"

Today is the first day of my obligatory "try and have fun with Grandma" assignment.

"You're late! What took you so long?" she snaps, standing in front of her brand-new wire-screen door wearing a peach floral dress that looks like it suffered a bomb blast in the war. Maybe I could take her clothes shopping. Don't women bond when they do that?

"Grandma, why are you standing out here?"

"You said you'd be here at ten o'clock!"

"It's only five minutes past."

"Go inside and kiss Grandpa and let's go, then."

I go inside; he grunts and gives me a dirty look from his chair next to the radio, which is blaring the greyhound races. I ignore his look, kiss him on his greasy cheek, puke (just kidding), and leave. He's always like that but usually worse. Grandma likes to blame the war for his behavior, but he didn't even leave the country. He just worked in an office while all the nice men went off to die.

"So what do you think of the car?" I ask Grandma as she gets in.

"It's a bit small, isn't it?"

"Yeah, but what would I need a big car for? Plus it's all I could afford," I say, looking up at the brand-new guttering on their house.

"Hmmm," she huffs.

We get to the supermarket and start shopping. Grandma buys twenty of everything that's on sale, complaining the whole way about the cost of living today and how people like me have no idea what it's like to be poor. I'm trying to see her as odd and quirky and fun, but the words *miserable old bitch* keep popping into my head.

We get to the checkout and she insults the girl at the cash register, who probably earns next to nothing. She tells the girl that she doesn't know how lucky she is to not be Grandma, with her phantom leukemia and other ailments, along with her poverty. I'm ready to throw Grandma in the shopping cart and push her off the top floor of the parking garage, but I try to stay calm.

"Are you hungry, Grandma? We could go to lunch. My treat."

"No, it's a waste of money."

"No, it's not. I'm taking you and that's that."

We've been in the restaurant for five minutes and already she's complained about the decor (too bright), the waitresses (too young), the food (you have to walk to it), the bathrooms (just because), but not the price. I made sure of that. Even though I'm paying, I knew she'd freak if we went anywhere expensive, so we're at an upmarket, value-for-money, all-you-can-eat place. I thought she'd be impressed with my thrifty ingenuity.

"They could at least bring the food to you."

"No, Grandma. The whole point is that you eat exactly what you like and as much as you can for one price. You can just keep going back."

"Not my idea of a restaurant."

"I thought you'd like it. Why don't you tell me what you want and I'll get it for you."

"Forget it, I'll get it myself," she says, pretending to have trouble getting out of her seat.

We get our food, sit back down (she groans as she does), and eat while I try to make conversation, eventually giving up.

I pay, we leave. I drive her home and put the groceries away, then turn to walk out the door.

"What, you're leaving? I thought you said you'd help me today," Grandma says, looking shocked.

"I have to be home by four o'clock," I tell her. Or I'll go crazy! "I'll be back soon."

I've got to find a way to pay back that two hundred dollars.

October 1985

"Tracy, I can't breathe," I tell her. I'm sitting on the verandah. I was getting ready to go to Julie's when an asthma attack hit me.

"Have you used your Ventolin?"

"Yes," I wheeze.

"Well, just breathe into a paper bag or something."

"This . . . is bad. . . . I . . . really can't . . . breathe."

"Well, if you'd stop panicking, you'd be all right. Just calm down, for God's sake."

She sounds just like Dad. He never believed me either. "It's all in your head," he used to say.

At least Mum was a believer. She explained that the

tubes in my lungs look like broccoli, and when I can't breathe, the broccoli becomes overcooked. Full of too much water, she'd say.

"Calm down!" Tracy yells.

How does someone calm down when they can't get any air into their lungs?

"Traaaaceyyyyyy," I wheeze. "This . . . is . . . one . . . of . . . the . . . worst . . . attacks . . . I've . . . ever . . . had . . . I'm . . . not . . . lying. I . . . think I . . . need . . . to go . . . to . . . the doctor."

"No, you don't. You've brought this on yourself. This isn't asthma, this is you being stupid. Just sit there and breathe," she says, slamming the wire-screen door behind her.

I puff on my Ventolin, breathe into a brown paper bag, and do the old arm-flapping exercises Dad used to make me do—"Arms out, breathe in, arms down, breathe out"—but nothing's working. Tracy gets impatient with me. This attack is just something she's not in the mood for today. She thinks that if I wanted to, I'd stop it. That like everything else I do, I'm doing this to her to make her life more miserable. It's really got nothing to do with me. I hope I die.

But my death would be another inconvenience. Funeral arrangements and all that. Funerals aren't cheap, and Ronald probably wouldn't give her any money for one. Not a necessary, justifiable expense, he'd say.

Well, I'm getting worse and I don't know what to do.

Tracy comes out every now and again and glares at me to tell me to breathe, but that only makes it worse.

"This is all in your head."

"It . . . isn't. Tracy . . . please . . . take . . . me . . . to . . . a hospital."

It's pathetic. I sound like Darth Vader after his balls have been cut off by Ronald's financial advisors.

I can't get any air past my throat, and I'm starting to feel dizzy and sick. My chest is aching from all the effort I'm putting into trying to push air down there. I'm a fish out of water. I'm terrified that If I move, the extra effort will kill me. What's the big deal about taking me to hospital? Does she really think I'm doing this on purpose? Why does she hate me so much? It's not my fault our life is like this.

It's a beautiful hot, sunny day. I'm going to die. This is it.

Here comes Chris in the VW. He's just dropped Trent off at one of his little friends' houses for the afternoon.

"Chris. I'm . . . having a bad . . . asthma . . . attack. I need . . . a doctor."

"Where's Tracy?"

"She's . . . inside. . . . She . . . doesn't . . . believe . . . me. . . . Please . . . tell her."

Chris goes inside and comes back out soon after with another brown paper bag.

"That won't work," I wheeze. "I've tried it. Please. I know . . . this is the . . . last . . . thing . . . Tracy needs . . .

right now but . . . it's . . . serious. I . . . really . . . can't . . . breathe. . . . I swear . . . I'm . . . begging. . . . Please take me . . . to . . . a . . . doctor."

Chris goes back inside. He's had enough of me too, and I don't blame him. I'm a burden, an inconvenience, a weight around their necks, a ball and chain. Their lives are so much harder than mine, and I make them harder just by being there. I know that, but I can't go anywhere yet. At least not until I finish school. But then . . . I can't leave Trent!

Another five minutes go by, and Chris comes out. By now I must be looking teary, pale, and authentic, because Chris's face changes and he goes inside and comes back out with the car keys.

I can hardly walk to the car. Hopefully that is helping authenticate my claim. Maybe Tracy is seeing this out the window and finally believes me.

Oh no! Tracy's locking the front door. She's coming too.

I'm sitting in the backseat. Chris is driving, and I'm wheezing even louder now, I can't help it. Tracy looks at me over her shoulder. "Shut up, Erin. You're only making it worse."

I'm in the children's ward at St. George Hospital. The hospital Dad was in. The hospital he died in. They don't have any room available in the older ward, and I don't mind. Actually, I like it. They're nicer to kids, and even though I'm now sixteen, they're nice to me, too. They treat me like every other child, despite the fact that I'm in an adult-size bed they've wheeled in. I wish I could shrink and be like every other little kid here.

I'm feeling really alone, but I sort of like it. I don't talk to the other kids, I keep to myself. I'm loving that I don't have to talk to anyone. I love that I don't have to do anything.

Sometimes I enjoy being self-pitying. I love lying here in my bed and imagining I'm the girl who has no one in the world. Some days I see a parent come in to visit his or her child and I think, "Poor little ol' me." Feeling sorry for myself is strangely comforting.

Every morning and afternoon a nurse comes in, turns me on my sides, and bashes my back and sides to clear up my lungs. She says they're full of accumulated junk. I love when she does that. I like being taken care of. It's like when I was little and Mum would make me Vegemite toast when I was sick.

Tracy continues to act like I'm such a fucking inconvenience for being sick. Her life is so much harder than mine, and how fucking dare I make it even harder! I don't expect sympathy, but she could be nicer.

"I couldn't help it, Tracy."

"It's okay," she says, letting me know it's not with her scowl.

I wish she wouldn't come. She ruins everything. I don't know why she even bothers.

Maybe she thinks she has to after not believing I was sick.

Tracy never brings anything, none of those sick-person goodies you can get at the hospital gift shop. She walks in with a dirty look on her face and never stays very long. On her way out after each visit she laughs and chats to the nurses in the corridor, acting like the concerned, caring older sister. Boy, that makes me mad.

On my fourth day there she brings Trent to see me. In my pink and blue bed with the children's pictures on the wall, I feel as little as he is.

He sits on the bed with me and asks when I'm coming home.

"As soon as the doctor lets me. I miss you so much, Trent."

"I love you, Erin," he says, and I try not to cry.

I hope Trent doesn't think I'm going to die and not come home. He doesn't seem too worried. Maybe he likes my not being at home. Maybe Tracy's calmer with me not there. Maybe it's a happy family without me.

I'm discharged after seven days. I wish I could stay here forever. To live in this world of meals on sectioned trays, air masks for when I can't breathe on my own, pink happy lambs jumping in a field on the wall, nice gentle nurses in crisp white uniforms who rub my tired, sore chest and bash the shit out of me.

A life like that would suit me just fine.

I'm back home.

Being in the hospital has got me thinking about Dad. We were told he died from a clot through the heart. I've never believed it. I think he killed himself and they don't want to upset me by telling me. Mum died on October 23 and Dad died on November 24. That's fishy to me. I reckon he lasted a month and then just couldn't take it anymore.

He was getting better; the doctors and nurses said so. Maybe he just didn't want to get better. Maybe he never wanted to come home and face it all: life without Mum, the guilt of thinking it was all his fault.

I need proof of how he died. I need to see his death certificate.

Because I'm up in the morning before everyone else with my studies, I can search for the death certificate then. I'm sure it's with the funeral books and stuff that's in the back cupboard. I find it right away. I hate this maroon vinyl book full of copies of the services and cards from flowers people sent to the funeral. It's so cheap and tacky. It could at least have been leather.

I unfold Dad's death certificate, leaving Mum's alone. I don't need or want to see that.

Yep, it says a clot through the heart. Can they lie about these things to the poor grieving children?

I still don't believe it. If it was a clot through the heart, I'm sure he willed it to go there.

He would have stupidly thought that the three of us would be better off without him to look after, without having to push our father around in a wheelchair. He probably thought we'd blame him for the accident. So the very next day, the one month anniversary of the accident, his body just said *Enough*.

If only he had known that the accident was partly my fault too, for thinking it in the first place . . . maybe things would be different.

January 1986

Tracy and Chris are getting a water bed and are insisting that I get one too. I'm happy to sleep on the foam and springs I've slept on my whole life. I don't even like swimming.

Tracy's a beautiful swimmer. She always won all of her races at school swim meets. Maybe that's why she wants a water bed. Maybe it's a way for her to think of good things at night, of a time when her life was happier. But I hate the water. Give me a flat, hard surface any day. Give me solid ground to sleep on. Sleeping is hard enough as it is.

"Tracy, I don't want one. I love my bed. You can't force me."

"You reckon?" she says, getting annoyed. "Trust me, Erin. You'll love a water bed."

"We can't afford it. It's a waste of money."

"There's a sale. God, why do you have to make things so difficult?" There are those gritted teeth again. "Besides, your mattress is old and lumpy,"

"I do all my homework and stuff on my bed," I point out.

"You can still do that on your new bed."

I raise my eyebrows. "I'll be able to write neatly while I'm sloshing around?"

Well, I'm getting a water bed and that's that. It's arriving today.

Maybe they heard somewhere that it's therapeutic or something. Like going back to the womb. Shrinks always talk about the womb when people are screwed up, don't they?

Chris has put the frame together, and I have to fill the big silver sack with water. So here I stand in my bedroom with the green backyard garden hose coming through my window pouring water into my room.

Every time I sit on the stupid thing, it sways and wobbles like jelly. I have nowhere to sit anymore. My bedroom is ruined. I used to love doing my homework on my bed, reading a book, or listening to my music. I could do that for hours. It was peaceful. A place where the world was still, a place where I could at least try to be still. I can't even do my homework on my bed anymore. Every time I try to write, the bed dips and my words fall off the page.

I've tried sleeping in the water bed for weeks now and it's not getting any better. How am I ever going to get used to this? I'm lost at sea for life.

I think I have post-traumatic stress syndrome. I've read about it in those stupid grief books. I've been carefully watching out for signs that I may be totally screwed up for life, that the accident has scarred me deeply. So deeply that I'd never be truly aware of it.

Well, I think I've found a sign.

One of my greatest childhood fears has come true: I've become a bed wetter.

I've gone my whole life without wetting the bed, and now, at the age of seventeen, my fear has been realized. Even five-year-old Trent doesn't wet the bed!

Am I really *that* screwed up?

My pajamas are soaking wet, my sheets are drenched. I change into some dry clothes and take the sheets off the bed. There's a lot of water. I couldn't have wet the bed. The stupid thing must have a leak. I knew this bed was going to be a disaster. This could be good. Maybe the bed's broken. Maybe I'll have to get rid of it!

There seem to be tiny holes in the silver plastic sack, near my pillow. How could have that happened? Hmmm. I did catch Trent playing with some of my sewing needles the other day. I hid them from him, thinking he might swallow one and die. The holes do look like pinpricks, though.

"Trent!" I'm calling him, pretty sure of what he's going to tell me. He's been curious about this bed since I got it. He comes bouncing into my room.

"Yes, Erin," he says in his husky little voice.

"Did you do anything to my new bed?"

"No," he says, trying to act innocent, which is not easy for a five-year-old who is guilty of something naughty.

"Are you sure?"

"No, I didn't do anything."

"I won't be mad at you. I promise." I smile, trying to make a joke of it so he'll tell me the truth. "Did you make holes in it?"

"I put pins in it," he says with an apprehensive smile. "I'm sorry."

"Trent!" I shout at him. "You don't do things like that!"

I'm angry and he's getting teary. I can't believe I'm doing it and I can't seem to help myself. I'm just like everyone else, just like an adult. I calm down and apologize.

"I'm sorry, Trent." I hug him. "But that was a naughty thing to do, wasn't it?"

"Yes," he says, frightened.

"But don't worry. I'll put a patch on it and it will be as good as new.

"I thought I'd wet the bed and would have to start wearing a diaper." I try to laugh with him, but he doesn't trust me now, and I don't blame him. I broke my promise about not getting mad at him.

He walks out looking sad.

I wish I had just wet the damn bed.

Tracy never thought her life would turn out like this. She was the queen of the disco. She was going to have a rich, handsome husband, a nice car, trips to tropical islands where she could coat herself with tanning oil, lots of jewelry stored in a huge safe in a fabulous house on the water. . . .

Well, she's on the water, all right, but this water is gray and murky, and she's not in her dream house. She's working as a waitress in a crummy waterside restaurant with plastic red and white checkered tablecloths.

She decided a while ago that she wanted to try a change from hairdressing because she's sick of all the whining people who tell her all their problems while she does their hair. "This job is perfect," she told me last week in a rare moment of bonding. "The hours are flexible, so I can still pick up Trent, and the boss is really nice."

Tracy has to work this Sunday, so Trent and I are going to visit her. It's fun driving with Trent in the car. Makes me feel like I'm taking charge of things.

When we walk into the restaurant, a small, frantic woman of about thirty is wiping down tables. She looks up and I'm shocked to see that it's Tracy. I try to smile like everything is okay, but it's not. She looks so old and sad and small and helpless and tired. Like life is crushing her and she has nothing left.

So this is her fantastic new job?

The whole mood of the restaurant is wrong. It's like the owners decided they would have a waterfront restaurant, not realizing the water was actually sludge. The building is on poles near the sand, but the water doesn't reach it. You can see the ocean way out in the distance through the floor-to-ceiling windows, but up close it's just puddles of gray water in the gray sand.

Seeing her do this job that is so far from her dreams just doesn't seem right. Apart from the night of the accident, I've never felt as bad for her as I do right now.

I never usually see her as a person, just as my bitch sister, but today she makes me want to cry.

When she gets a lunch break, we go outside and walk in the mushy sand. Trent runs and splashes, oblivious to what an awful place we're in. He giggles and makes us laugh the kind of laugh that could turn to crying at any minute.

Tracy never wants to talk, but today I get the feeling she might. So I try to start up a conversation.

"So, do you like the job?" I ask.

"Yeah, it's okay, I suppose," she says, looking defeated but trying to hide it.

"It won't always be like this, you know," I say.

"Trent, don't go too far!" she yells as he runs away from us.

"Tracy, I'll get a great career and make enough money for all of us." That didn't come out right. It sounds like I think she can't. I seem to always think I can be the family savior, not realizing that maybe she's insulted by that.

I want to tell her I know how she suffers. I want to tell her I'll be a better sister from now on. I want to tell her that everything will be all right one day. We'll get through it and find a way to a better life, a life where we won't have to struggle anymore. A life where she doesn't have to do stuff that's so far from who she really is.

I know there are a lot of people out there doing bum jobs they hate. I just think a girl who loses her parents and has to take care of two younger siblings without much money or help from anyone deserves better.

I want everything to be the way it is in the movies. I want to hug her, but I don't. I want us to share and cry, but we don't.

It's all awkward and wrong and we couldn't be more different.

So we walk through the sludge before she has to go back and wipe tables and clean up after the lunch crowd.

I can't stand seeing her do that with her apron on. It's not who she is. I know that much.

"Tracy, Erin, I need to go to the bathroom."

"That's okay, Trent, we're at the beach," Tracy says.

The three of us have come to the beach—a real beach this time—to get out of the house and try something new together. It's a perfect day. The sun's shining, the sand's hot and white, and the blue water is clear and still enough for a nonswimmer like me to swim in.

"But there's nowhere to go," Trent says, crossing his muscular little legs.

"That's easy, just go in the water," I say. The nearest restroom is way too far to walk to in time.

"Really . . . no one will mind?"

"Everybody does it at the beach."

"Oh," he says, and he's off and running, holding on to his swimming trunks . . . but . . . he's stopped with the water up to his ankles.

"Why isn't he going in?" I ask Tracy as she reapplies her tanning oil.

"I don't know. Maybe he's scared," she says, laughing at his cuteness.

It's great sitting here next to her laughing and oiling up. It's like we're a couple of girlfriends out for the day.

"He's never been scared of the water before," I say, watching him.

"That's true."

"Oh my God, he's pulling his willy out of his pants!" I'm really laughing now. He must not realize we meant he should be totally in the water before he starts peeing.

We look at each other and know we should go and tell Trent he's doing it wrong, but it's too much fun watching the arc of water going from his little body to the sea.

Tracy laughs. "Fine big sisters we are!"

Every time she laughs, I feel the laugh inside me. It's wonderful and corny and great.

We keep watching and try not to laugh at our little brother standing and peeing on a crowded beach. People must think he has terrible parents with even more terrible manners.

I love times like this, when Tracy and I are laughing and Trent is happy. It's like we're a real family and nothing bad has ruined us.

Maybe there's hope for us yet.

June 1986

We're leaving Knock Crescent.

Sorry, house, we've sold you to the highest bidder. It's time to get away from all the bad memories, Tracy says. I'm not sure I'm ready to leave. Tracy and Chris have decided to get married and don't want to start married life in this sad old house. Who can blame them?

It's strange. All I've wanted to do is leave this rotten house, and now all I want to do is stay . . . or do I? Will I forget everything if I leave? I want to forget. But I don't want to. I don't know what I want. I know I can't live here anymore. It's like the sadness lives here with us, and if we stay, it stays. I don't know if we'll be happy anywhere, but we've got more of a chance someplace else.

Am I leaving Mum and Dad? Am I leaving the good times behind forever? I can't remember them anyway. It's like they happened to another girl.

Will I remember what my room looks like? Will I remember Mum and Dad's room? Actually, I really could live without that. Will Trent be sad or will he not really care? I still don't know if he's aware of what's going on. It doesn't help that Tracy won't let us talk to him about it. She's even started telling Trent to call her "Mum" and Chris "Dad" in front of people at his school to prevent confusion with his friends. What about Trent's confusion? It's like our parents never existed. I know it feels like that sometimes, but we should keep some memories for Trent, shouldn't we?

What will it be like to come back to this street and see other people in our house?

I doubt I'll ever come back.

Goodbye, Knock Crescent.

Goodbye, Dad's cheap ugly bar made of fake bendy bricks that curve with the heat of a hair dryer. Goodbye, ugly metal clothesline that Mum used to hang her undies on, behind bath towels so no one could see them.

Goodbye, my very first bedroom, with your pink and purple flowered wallpaper. Goodbye, beautiful cement inground pool. Dad was so happy that he finally worked his way up from an aboveground circular plastic pool to you. Goodbye, lemon tree; you were so generous when I decided I wanted to go all out and have a real American lemonade stand out the front. Goodbye, Mum's dining set. Friends are looking after you for a while, until we know what we want to do permanently. Goodbye, Mum and Dad's room. I'm sorry, but I'm locking your door and throwing away the key.

Time to start again. Time to stop holding on to the past. Time to make things better.

Goodbye, Knock Crescent. You really did live up to your name as a dead end.

I was in hell, but now I'm in L.

We've moved into an old sandstone house fifteen minutes away from Knock Crescent.

My room is L-shaped, and even though it's tiny, it's really cool-looking. It's almost like having two rooms. And it's right at the back corner of the house.

"Gee, they've put you in the closet," Julie says when she comes over for the first time.

Tracy and Chris have the room at the front of the house and Trent is in the room directly opposite them, so it's like I have my own space. I can almost pretend I have my own little apartment.

I think things are going to be better here. There are no sad attachments. The living room is just a living room and the kitchen is just a boring old kitchen. Tracy's still talking in Tracyspeak, but it's not as disturbing in this house.

It's just a house and nothing more.

I wonder who's living in our home.

Now that we have a new house, we decide it's time to get some of Mum and Dad's furniture back. But when

Tracy calls Noelene, who's been storing Mum's prized dining room set, she actually refuses to part with it. I can't believe it, so when Tracy, Chris, and Trent are out, I call Noelene myself.

"Our mother loved that dining set and glass cabinet," I tell my mother's old friend. "They hold so many memories for us."

"We really can't give them up now," she says. I can't believe her nerve.

A couple of days later I work up the courage to drive to Noelene's house. I hate to do it, but it seems like my only option. I feel pretty certain that if Noelene sees me in person, she won't be able to say no.

I'm standing in her dining room staring at our table and chairs.

"Look, Erin, I'm sorry, but we've designed our whole living room around these pieces," Noelene explains with a shrug. Is this the same woman who used to laugh with my parents? Whose house we used to go to for family barbecues? Whose friendship meant a lot to Mum?

"But you promised," I blurt out. I am so angry. Mum would be crushed.

Noelene shakes her head and walks toward the door. "I'm sorry. No."

I'm seventeen and powerless to do anything else.

And that's that.

October 23, 1986

I've got to keep busy.

1:00 p.m.: Mum and Dad were leaving for the cemetery at exactly this time three years ago.

7:00 p.m.: No, this is too much. Even after three years! What is wrong with me?

Trent and I watch *The Wizard of Oz* and I try to forget.

November 24, 1986

Don't think about it. Don't think about it.

1:00 p.m.: Three years ago today, Chris came and got me from school.

Just keep smiling. The day will be over soon.

December 1986

This is it.

It's the last day of school, and we're clearing out our lockers.

No more five a.m. wake-up study sessions, no more religious debates with Mrs. C-J, no more green and white uniforms, no more therapy sessions with pseudo-counselor Merril, no more assemblies, no more laughs with my friends during lunch . . .

I've studied hard and gotten good grades, and now it's time to get my reward. But before all that, it's time to be a brainless idiot one last time in the traditional end-of-school egg and flour fight with Narwee Boys' High. The teachers don't like it but figure it's pretty harmless and it would be more work to try and stop us.

It's eleven-thirty a.m. and the boys are already throwing eggs at the school windows.

Being the educated girls that we are, Julie and I have four dozen eggs and several bags of flour in my car ready to go. We run to the parking lot, dodging eggs. One splats on my car's passenger window just as Julie slams the door shut.

We drive down the backstreets behind school. Julie has a carton of eggs in her lap and a bag of flour at her feet. We're speeding past boys in trucks already covered in flour. Ha! So some girls are out here with us. All right!

We're invincible, doing forty miles an hour in reverse as a car full of boys heads our way. I swerve and they miss us, and we're off again.

"*I'm a maniac, maniac,*" I sing in true *Flashdance* style as Julie yells out the window. We're carefree and careless; nothing can touch us.

School's over and we made it. Nothing matters but eggs and flour, flour and eggs . . . and then: "Shit, it's one-thirty!" Julie shrieks. "The final assembly starts soon!"

I accelerate to sixty miles an hour to get back in time.

"Do I have any egg in my hair?" I ask as we speed back into the school parking lot.

"A little bit, but you can hardly tell."

We hop out of my white car. Dripping with egg yolks, it looks like one big scramble.

Covered in egg and flour, Julie and I walk into the assembly hall. It's filled with parents and teachers and other students covered in flour.

We sit with Julie's parents and run up onstage when our names are called. I thought it would be horrible to not have Mum and Dad here, but it seems that maybe I'm getting used to their not being around, because I'm not feeling too bad.

So, it's time to say goodbye to the teachers we like, and see you later to our friends, who we will see later, and get back into my car and drive away.

No more getting ready for the future—the future is here.

My new life starts now.

I've only been out of school a few weeks and I have a job. My dream job. Well, my number two dream job, after acting. But as Mum used to say, a person must eat, and most actors don't, apparently. They can't afford to. Maybe that's why they're all so skinny. Anyway, I don't want to act anymore. I can't, for some reason.

I'm going to be a journalist for the biggest newspaper company in Australia. I passed an entrance exam that News Limited gives to prospective candidates, and they hired me. I'm going to be working in their big offices in the center of Sydney, writing for the *Australian,* the *Daily Telegraph,* and more.

I can't afford to go to college like most of my friends,

but now I'm thinking that this is even better. Maybe things do happen for a reason. If I work really hard, I have a chance to make enough money for all of us.

It's the day of Tracy and Chris's wedding.

We're outside at a restaurant by the water. It's beautiful. It's nothing like the one Tracy worked at (thankfully, she quit).

Chris is wearing a white tuxedo. I'm in my black satin bridesmaid dress, walking in front of Trent and Tracy, who today looks like she belongs in the rich Beverly Hills. It's the beautiful, before-the-accident Tracy. Trent is walking her down the aisle.

When the celebrant asks who gives Tracy away, I look down and smile at Trent, who is so proud in his little white tuxedo with a red rose in the lapel. I nudge him and he answers, "I do."

All the guests smile and make that *awww* sound you hear when someone as cute as Trent says something sweet. Grandma starts her usual dramatic crying, and Auntie Connie walks over to quiet her down.

It's a beautiful wedding and it goes off without a hitch—until they read the telegrams. There's one from Mum and Dad saying they wish they could be here. Tracy and I stare at each other, wondering what the hell is going on. Then Chris's mum smiles at us and we realize it's her doing. We're furious. We were trying to leave Mum and Dad out of this and just enjoy the day.

The music starts and we dance and try and forget about it, and then it's time to say goodbye.

We all stand in a circle to kiss them as they go off in their white limo. When Tracy gets to Trent, she grabs him and starts crying.

"Come on, Tracy," I say gently.

"I can't leave him," she sobs, and Trent pats her head.

"I'll be all right," he says.

Auntie Connie comes over and hugs them both, and Tracy lets go.

Now that Chris and Tracy are married, I think maybe it's time I leave. Time to let them get on with their lives and for me to get on with mine.

April 1987

There are twelve of us newbies at the paper, and every day we attend training sessions in things like shorthand and typing. My official title is "copy-person." When we're not in class, we work different shifts, sitting in a row near the editor's office.

When a journalist or subeditor yells out, "Copy!" one of us jumps and runs to that person's desk to get them coffee, lunch, photos from the photo library, or information from the cuts library, which houses maps, encyclopedias, books, and all the stories that have ever appeared in the paper.

I love it.

Julie and I find an apartment to share. It's tiny, but it's

ours. Moving away from Trent was the hardest part, but we're only five minutes away.

But not for long.

"Chris and I have decided to leave," Tracy tells me. She's come to visit me at my new apartment. I'm sitting at Mum's sewing machine making some serious journalist clothes for my new career. Today I'm hemming a black pinstripe pantsuit.

"I can see why you'd want a nicer house," I say.

"No, I mean . . . we're leaving Sydney. We're going to move to Queensland."

This surprises me. "What? What about Trent?"

"He'll come too."

I drop the fabric. "What are you talking about? You can't! That's ten hours away."

"Erin, we'll never get ahead. We'll never be able to afford a place of our own here. It's too expensive . . . unless we want to live in a dumpy suburb out in woop-woop."

What she's saying makes sense, but it's not what I want to hear. "But Tracy, can't you hold on? I'm going to start making good money soon."

She shakes her head. "Erin, that will take years."

"Not if I work really hard. I—"

"Erin, you were making more at Cookie Man," Tracy says, and it's true. "It's going to take years before you're making decent money. We can't wait for you to climb up the ladder, and I don't expect you to try and do this for all of us."

"But—"

Tracy fiddles with her pocketbook and sighs, and I

realize how tired she looks. "We have to go, Erin. I need to get away from here."

"But I don't want you to leave. And please don't take Trent so far away."

"You can come if you want," she tells me, looking away.

I have a feeling she's hoping I'll say no.

I don't know what to do. I've got my job and my apartment. Everything I know is here. Tracy tells me that they'll be moving in a month's time. When she tells me that she and Chris only just decided to move, I believe her. Tracy's never been one to make long-term plans.

But I am.

What do I want to do with my life? If I stay here and change my mind, I can always leave my job and move to Queensland. But if I leave my job, move, and realize it was the wrong decision, I'll be stuck.

If I move with them, who knows if I'll find an opportunity like the one I have now at the newspaper? Sure, I'll be there with Trent. But is that enough? I want to give him more.

I don't know what to do. Do I stay or do I go?

I stay. After talking it over with Julie and driving myself bonkers thinking about it, I decide that some time apart might be the best thing for me and Tracy. It might even make us closer. I don't want to quit my job. And if it gets to be too much being away from Trent, I can always change my mind.

Before they leave, I call Ronald. It's been months since

I've spoken with him. When he answers the phone, I take a deep breath and launch into my request. I'm calling him because I need some money, and any pride I had vanished long ago. I want to take a trip to London. He knows that Tracy is moving and I'm not, and I've got a small kernel of hope in my chest that maybe he'll take pity on me—the one left behind—and be willing to give me enough to pay for my airfare and a few weeks' spending money. I figure I'll start off big, and if it turns out that he'll only give me a few hundred dollars, that's a few hundred more than I started with.

My uncle shocks me. "Hold it right there," he interrupts happily. "We can take that out of your money."

Did I just hear right? "Really?" I don't get it. He's always saying no to things much more important than this. What's changed?

"You've been through a lot, Erin. You deserve it."

"Well, thanks," I say, caught off guard. "Thanks, Ronald."

We make a bit of small talk. And then he drops the bomb. "Look, Erin. About your money. I'm in a bit of hot water."

"What's wrong?" I ask.

"I've done something I shouldn't have. Just between you and me, I borrowed some of your money. Mind you, I had full intentions of paying it back."

Is he kidding? After all the times we called him, begging for money to help pay our bills, to help keep us going—to buy Trent Christmas presents, for God's sake—

he "borrowed" some? What a low-life bastard. Am I really related to this asshole?

I want to yell and scream, but I don't. I've got to act like this isn't a big deal to me so he'll open up more. I want to know everything, every detail. He won't tell me if I start yelling.

The journalist in me takes over. "How much money have you used?" I ask, and grab a notepad and pen.

"I don't know exactly. Probably about . . . say . . . twenty thousand dollars."

"Twenty thousand dollars?" I blurt out more loudly than I intended. Stay calm, Erin, stay calm.

"Erin, promise me you won't tell anyone. Promise. You can't tell Tracy."

"I promise." Yeah, right! "Does Peter know?"

"Erin, please don't tell him. . . . I've . . . I've used some money for my business."

"Business? What business?"

"I've—I've been buying old tractors, refurbishing them, and selling them."

"So where's that money? The money from the sale of the tractors then?"

"I put it back into the business."

"Why not just put it back into our trust account?" I ask.

"That's not how business works," he explains, as if I should know this.

"Well, how's the business that has our money in it doing, then?"

"Well, you know. These things take time."

"Ronald! How's the business doing?"

There's a long, uncomfortable silence.

"Well?" I prompt.

"Um . . . it's not so good, actually, but things will get better. I promise."

"So where the hell is our money?"

He doesn't answer, and I'm getting into a panic.

"And what about the money from the sale of the house? And the life insurance Mum and Dad had? Where is it?"

I can't believe this.

Ronald keeps talking. "Erin, they'll probably throw me in jail. I don't know what to do. God, I'm in a lot of trouble now. I suppose when you dip into the cash box you've got to expect your fingers to get burnt."

"Is that worse than having your balls cut off?" I want to ask, but I'm playing it cool.

"A trustee isn't allowed to invest money in his own business schemes to make himself richer," I say hotly. I might be only eighteen, but I know that much. "You were just supposed to take care of it for us and give it to us when we needed it." Not that he ever did.

"I'm sorry, Erin, I'm sorry. Please don't tell the lawyers about this."

My hand is gripping the phone. "So is there any money there for my trip?"

"How much do you need?" he asks.

"A thousand dollars," I say boldly.

"I could probably manage five hundred."

I'm seething even more than I was when he told me about his "business."

"I'll send you a check right away," he continues. "Thanks for being so understanding about this, Erin. I'll work it all out. Don't worry."

Oh, I'm not worried, Ronald, because I'm going to work it all out. I'm going to get it back from you and then come and cut your balls off myself!

I say goodbye, hang up, and put my pencil down.

What the hell am I going to do?

Is it really so bad that Ronald blew our inheritance? It's a pretty horrible way to get money. We wouldn't have it if Mum and Dad didn't die.

What the hell am I thinking? It's the principle of the thing. You don't take money from your dead sister's children. How could he?

How am I going to get it back? Maybe I could write a story for the newspaper: *Uncle Swindles Parentless Children*. There's a lawyer at the paper who handles all the legal stuff for the company. He could give me advice. And I have to tell Tracy at some point.

Retaliating against our deadbeat uncle is one thing we can definitely do as sisters.

Tracy, Chris, and Trent are leaving today. They took Trent to say goodbye to Grandma and Grandpa the other day, and now it's my turn.

We didn't have a farewell dinner or anything, because Tracy didn't want to make a big deal out of it. *"Things are still a big deal whether you ignore them or not,"* I want to say, but we've had that conversation before, and I have to accept that we just think differently when it comes to that kind of stuff.

I'm standing on the footpath outside my apartment building waiting for their van to pull up. They traded in the beloved VW Beetle for it. I feel sick to my stomach. I can't believe they're leaving. After all these years of fighting to stay together and generally just fighting, it's coming to an end. Or is this the beginning? Will it be good for us to have time apart? I don't know. I just know I love them so much and can't stand the thought of them leaving. I never thought I'd say that about Tracy after all we've put each other through. I guess blood *is* thicker than water in lots of ways. There's a tie there that just won't break no matter how much it's pulled. So does it really matter that it's going to be stretched for miles and miles?

The van pulls up. Here come my tears. I've got to stop crying—Tracy hates tears.

I manage to dry my eyes before the van stops and Trent jumps out. My heart flops around in my chest. No, he can't leave, he can't. What will I do without him? What will I be without his sweet little smile? He runs to me and I pick him up.

"Oh, Trent, I love you so, so much. You know that, right?" I can't see him through my tears.

"I love you too, Erin," he says, and puts his head on my shoulder. Now I am sobbing.

Will he forget me? Will he forgive me? Will he miss me? Will he think I'm dead? Does he know enough to care? Am I doing the right thing? Are they?

It's strange, but everything seems so simple all of a sudden.

We're family no matter what. Mum and Dad's not being here can't change that. If anything, their absence makes us feel more like family.

"Bye, Trent. I love you. Bye, Chris."

And then I look at Tracy, really look at her for the first time this morning.

"Bye, Tracy. I . . . I . . . love you."

And she looks at me and says the same, and I think she means it.

Maybe apart we can finally come together.

Afterword

Tracy and Chris live by the beach in Queensland, Australia, and have two teenage daughters, my darling nieces Shae and Bree.

Trent has a daughter, Michaella, who lives with her mother in America, not far from her devoted Auntie Erin. In 2006 Trent was married in a traditional ceremony in Japan. He and his Japanese wife, Mayu, live happily by the beach in Queensland as well.

In late 1987 I hired a lawyer (Tracy didn't want to be involved) and eventually got most of our money back, much more than Ronald admitted to taking. A couple of years later, at the funeral of a distant relative, Ronald said to Tracy, "Tell Erin I forgive her." I have not seen him since. I made many attempts to have a relationship with Peter, but he was not responsive.

My grandfather died eight years after the accident. My grandmother wore a hot pink terry-cloth tracksuit to his funeral and introduced the few mourners to each other over the open grave as the minister tried to conduct the service. She died a few years later.

Auntie Connie and Uncle Steele still live in the same house in the cul-de-sac and are as wonderful and caring as ever. I visit them whenever I go back to Australia. They, and their children, generously shared many memories with me for this book, as did Julie. We had lost contact until I searched for her in 2001. Through her mother I found her living with her boyfriend in Sydney. We have since been writing letters back and forth and she is once again a wonderful blessing in my life.

And me? I met the love of my life five years after the accident. One day late in 1988 the newspaper sent me out on assignment with a young photographer, Adam Knott. In an instant I knew he was someone special. We have been together ever since.

Being married to a photographer has been quite an experience. I have done many strange things for the sake of art. I've worn a wolf's-head mask while standing naked on a Malibu beach, worn an elephant's trunk as well as a giant bug's head in public, been covered from head to toe with shaving cream, dressed up as Winnie-the-Pooh, and generally been a more than willing guinea pig. In the midst of all of this Adam also documented my grief and tears and laughter—all the things I could not have gotten through without him by my side.

So, am I still a journalist? Well, it turned out that journalism wasn't for me. One day when I was coming back from an assignment in a taxi, a barrage of police cars swooped in on a man in the street, forcing him to the ground. The photographer with me jumped out of the cab.

"Quick, Erin, let's go."

My reply? "Oh, I think I'll go back to the office and have a cappuccino."

It turned out the man was on Australia's Ten Most Wanted list and the incident was front-page news. Lucky for me, the photographer was Adam and the paper never found out they could have had a journalist on the scene!

Realizing I wasn't a true journalist, I took what I considered my "blood money" from the accident and decided I had to do something special with it. Something my mother would be proud of. So I went to see the world she never saw. I snorkeled in Indonesia, bummed around India, trekked in Nepal, rode a motorcycle off a wharf in Greece (oops!), and backpacked through Europe.

Upon my return I wanted to do something more creative and was awarded a scholarship to fashion school, which led to the prestigious job of counting buttons for a top designer for a year.

Discontented with our careers in Australia, Adam and I decided to try our luck in America. We arrived in Los Angeles on October 23, 1995 (ironically, the anniversary of the accident). We were illegal aliens for eighteen months until our green card applications went through, living on potatoes and free packets of salt, pepper, and ketchup. To this day I can make a mean potato dish!

Adam became a successful magazine photographer, and I worked for a well-known female fashion designer who started each day doing naked yoga beside my desk. Tired of the view, I started my own label and sold my designs while working as a freelance tailor/stylist for celebrity photo shoots. I sat on a famous Hollywood producer's bed first thing in the morning as he wiped the sleep from his eyes before being measured for his new silk pajamas, almost wet my pants on an Annie Leibovitz *Vanity Fair* shoot because I was not allowed to go to the bathroom in case the comedian-turned-major-movie-star had to go, and was hoisted up on a crane and left dangling while a photographer checked how the light would look when a certain TV star was wearing the dress they had me wear. I knew it was time to quit when I had to kneel at the feet of a famous actress to hem her dress a day before the Oscars. I felt invisible and small and decided I had to do something else.

Adam had been urging me for years to write about my experience, but I resisted, thinking my story was too boring for a whole book. Then one day I said, "Oh, what the hell, I can knock it out in six months!" That was eight years ago.

While writing the book, I worked as Adam's photo assistant. He would photograph celebrities in their homes and I would set up lights and take light readings, yawning the whole time, tired from the long days of writing. "Erin, you can't yawn in front of the celebrity," Adam would whisper on jobs. "You're meant to look interested." Eventually he fired me. What a relief!

So I got a job at a Los Angeles bookstore hosting events for authors, dreaming of one day hosting my own.

I hope I have done my parents justice, because without the solid foundation they gave me before they died, I would never have gotten this far.

—*Erin Vincent,* MARCH 2007